Life is Meditation; Meditation is Life!

A Practical Guide to the "Emancipation Proclamation" of the Ānāpānasati Sutta and Loving-Kindness Meditation

Venerable Bhante Vimalaraṁsi
Mahāthera

Other Books by Bhante Vimalaraṁsi

The Ānāpānasati Sutta   1995
Breath of Love   2011
Moving Dhamma Vol. 1   2012
The Dhamma Leaf Series   2014

ISBN-13: 978-1495278334
ISBN-10: 1495278336

Contents

Author's Introduction

This revolutionary book is offered as clear and precise way of practicing and understanding what meditation is and how to do it according to the earliest known texts from the Buddha.

The author discovered the simplicity and practicality of the Buddha's Dhamma, when he began exploring the suttas of the earliest texts available!

This was done by letting go of most commentarial writing like the Vissudhi Magga (The Path of Purification) by Venerable Buddhaghosa.

When putting those commentaries back on the shelf where they belong, I then began investigating the original texts with much enthusiasm, because it was there that I found the true pearls of wisdom that can be used with real success in daily life in a very practical way.

This was when I studied and practiced deeply the differences between what I had been taught by the commentaries and what I discovered in the texts before ever showing this amazing path to others.

This is the third edition of the *Ānāpānasati Sutta* and has been expanded to include the Loving-Kindness Meditation instructions. It also gives more detailed explanations of HOW Dependent Origination and the Four Noble Truths are the very Backbone and Footsteps of the Tathāgata Path to awakening.

By teaching straight from the suttas many students have gained deep meditation practice and understanding of why they meditate and how to have a happy mind all of the time. This means not only while doing their formal sitting practice but also throughout all aspects of their life.

By going back to the foundation practice of meditation and using the small adjustments in the technique of meditation, the Buddha shows how your practice can really take off and become successful.

This book shows just how to do this easily and with excellent results, when followed exactly.

Bhante Vimalaraṁsi, Abbot

UIBDS – Dhamma Sukha Meditation Center

Annapolis, Missouri

Foreword

It is a great gift to be born as a human being within the time frame of the Buddha Dispensation when the Four Noble Truths are still around and this Doorway of Peace is open to us.

What a wonderful time to take a journey in spirituality.

In this year, 2014, The Buddha-Dhamma is still a very real and priceless treasure that can be clearly shared to reveal the truth that, in itself, reality is benign and that by experiencing and understanding this completely, we can regain control over our emotions and reclaim stability in life.

Isn't this one of the reasons we go on this spiritual journey, to regain balance and happiness in our everyday life?

Once you have discovered this kind of balance, life is never the same and each day becomes a day to give thanks and to take refuge in the Buddha, the Dhamma, and the Sangha for preserving this magnificent treasure of Peace.

When human beings learn the Dhamma, in an easy to remember usable fashion, they can embrace it and use it as a system for relief from suffering.

Then we naturally begin to open up an Ocean of Compassion that exists inside each one of us.

It has always been there, but most of us are moving too fast to learn about it.

The practices discussed in this book can brighten any position in a chosen career path, expand the potential use of mind, increase productivity considerably, and offer tranquility, happiness, and peace.

This inherent compassion is often released from within us when we are told the true nature of everything and taught how to see it for ourselves.

Of course, as you read, you must earnestly embrace and practice what you read and be bold enough to pursue it.

The first edition of this little book was printed in 1995 and since then it continues to spread through its own energy worldwide.

Hundreds of thousands of copies now exist in multiple languages.

It's even been used in universities abroad as a basic handbook for meditation.

The Author

The author, Most Venerable "Bhante" Vimalaraṁsi, is a Mahā Thera Buddhist monk with over forty years of meditation experience.

He presides over the "United International Buddha Dhamma Society" (UIBDS), which he founded in 2003.

He then founded the first location for Dhamma Sukha Meditation Center in the forest in Missouri, U.S.A. and became the first American Abbot there.

In late 2003, Bhante began overseeing the first online support program for students who had trained with him. This program is still very active in helping the Buddha-Dhamma grow.

In 2004 the current center location was purchased, a plan for the study and training was laid out, and online retreats and training began.

In 2006, by invitation, Bhante attended a nomination tour to Japan in consideration of his becoming the first Senior Level American Buddhist monk to represent the United States of America in the largest World Buddhist Council in Japan.

In 2008, upon approval of the nominating committees, he was officially inaugurated as the lifetime U.S. Representative and attended the 5th World Buddhist Summit in Japan (WBC) based in Kato and Kyoto, Japan.

This is the world's largest Buddhist organization openly dedicated to researching, practicing, preserving, and teaching as closely as possible the earliest foundation teachings of the Buddha-Dhamma.

During the 5th Buddhist summit in Kato, Japan, Venerable Vimalaraṁsi officially announced the founding of the **Buddhist American Forest Tradition.** This tradition recognizes the BUDDHA as its only teacher and its commitment to the equal training of men and women in its meditation and ordination programs.

Furthermore, in 2014 Venerable Vimalaraṁsi announced that the sect of Buddhism that he represents is now the **Suttavadin** sect. He has resurrected the name of a branch of Theravada Buddhism that only followed the Suttas.

Any guides produced now or in the future within this tradition are committed to being the supporting spiritual guides for this line and the Buddha is looked upon as the main teacher and informer, no one else.

Gradually, a study center, dedicated to the research, practice, preservation, and teaching of the Buddha-

Dhamma as close to its fundamental roots as possible, is emerging.

"This tradition works in today's world and is currently spreading Dhamma worldwide for the welfare and happiness of all people."

As a meditator, Venerable Vimalaraṁsi was ordained in the Burmese Forest Tradition by the late Most Venerable Sayadaw U Sīlanandabhivamsa.

He was then trained by some of the most famous teachers in the world in Theravada, Mahāyana, and Tibetan Buddhism.

He spent over twenty years following commentarial explanations and instructions in places like Mahāsi center and Chanmayay Yeiktha in Burma.

For many years, he meditated very successfully within the Asian framework before he personally began to investigate and compare the commentarial and sutta instructions for meditation.

Following the advice of an Elder Sri Lankan Mahāthera monk, Bhante found that some outstanding meditation results are still possible by stepping away from the commentarial explanations (mainly the Vissudhi Magga) and following the sutta instructions more precisely.

He realized that these meditation results were not the same as what people had understood from the commentarial instructions.

Therefore, he put aside the commentary and deeply studied the words of the Buddha, in the earliest known texts available and pursued his practice of meditation.

This paid off! Why? Because as it says The Mahākaccanabhaddekaratta Sutta (Majjhima Nikāya sutta number 133:9):

"For knowing, the Blessed One knows; seeing, he sees; he is vision, he is knowledge, he is the Dhamma, he is the holy one; he is the sayer, the proclaimer, the elucidator of meaning, the giver of the Deathless, the Lord of the Dhamma, the Tathāgata."

For over fifteen years now, Venerable has dedicated himself to teaching and preserving what the Buddha taught and is willing to train anyone who would dare to ask the following questions and pursue the answers:

- Did the Buddha actually find a way out of daily suffering?
- If he did find this, how did he do it?
- Did he identify clearly this suffering and show how it arises and passes away?
- Did he leave instructions and describe results we can achieve?
- Can anyone practice this path in this day and time and achieve similar various degrees of success?
- As a layperson, what difference can it make in daily life, at school or work or concerning interactions and worldly affairs?

This practice brings that to reality

Meditation is Life! Life is Meditation!

The Book

[Please take note that all sutta sections are printed in BOLD TYPE throughout this book.]

This book mainly examines The Ānāpānasati Sutta from the Majjhima Nikāya: The Middle Length Discourses as translated by Ven. Bhikkhu Ñāṇamoli and Ven. Bhikkhu Bodhi, published by Wisdom Publications, supplemented by information from other suttas.

This sutta teaches us Mindfulness of Breathing through using *Tranquil Wisdom Insight Meditation* (TWIM) or samatha/vipassanā.

When clearly understood, these same instructions can be applied when using Metta (Loving-Kindness) as the object of meditation.

In this edition of the book both objects of meditation, the Breath and Metta, are explained.

To experience the benefits of using this practice, we strongly advise you to choose ONLY ONE of these objects, the Breath OR Metta, and stick with it while you follow *only* the instructions given, very closely, for a minimum of one month.

Do not change meditations, because it will confuse the mind.

Don't add anything to the instructions or subtract anything while you are doing this meditation.

Let go of all other meditation practices to see how well this works.

If you have been practicing using the Breath for a long time, you may want to start at the beginning again by using Metta when you do this experiment.

This will help overcome old bad habits that you may have already developed and bring up new habits that will reveal true progress on the path.

The instructions for the meditation are repeated several times throughout the Pāli Canon using the same identical words.

This is NOT a form of prose.

Make no mistake about this! This is an ancient form of training.

Certain phrases within a sutta re-emphasize the importance of valuable instructions.

Thus you find a routine repetition concerning what you should ingrain in your mind to work with, when you do the meditation.

Think of this as:

1. listening to what the teacher is going to tell you,
2. listening to the teacher tell you directly, and,
3. listening to the teacher tell you what they just told you!

By that time, you know it!

By listening in this way, you will remember when you practice it.

In the past, some have said that there are more than forty objects of meditation mentioned in the Suttas.

However, on closer examination, you will find that all objects of meditation use the same technique of relaxing the tightness caused by craving in the same way to reach the same goal of understanding.

The spine of the Buddha's teaching is discovered by seeing and understanding clearly the impersonal process of Dependent Origination and the Four Noble Truths.

With these two pieces understood, the Dhamma can be fully realized.

This book is about using the breath or mettā and smiling and relaxing as the object of the meditation, to help you reach that lofty goal.

In only a few days you can see how it is truly possible to let go of suffering.

Monastics and lay people that have put forth a sincere effort to follow these instructions precisely make remarkable strides in understanding the Buddha Dhamma quickly.

If you are an experienced meditator, but are discouraged by your overall progress, this practice has the effect of teaching you how to refine your meditation perfectly.

Bhante manages to bring the teachings to life right here in America, using clear, simple English words.

Until now, learning from the texts has not been easy to understand for many Western and Asian lay people and teachers alike. Therefore, it becomes evident that the repetition found in this book is there to drive home the most important information in the simplest way possible.

It is hoped that by reading the book you will gain insight into what the Buddha actually taught. It will be different from what you have heard elsewhere so please keep an open mind. Try it before you judge it.

The Buddha said to all of us to "Come and See" how it works in the Kalama Sutta. This book is your open invitation.

"Life is Meditation; Meditation is Life!"

Ven. Sister Khema, November, 2013
Chairperson – United International Buddha Dhamma Society, Inc.
Dhamma Sukha Meditation Center and Anāthapindika's Study Park.

www.dhammasukha.org

Introduction: An Open Invitation

**Namo Tassa Bhagavato Arahato
Sammā Sambuddhasa**

Many people are now on a spiritual search for a path that leads their mind to peace, happiness, and openness.

They discovered that the norms of the world, which emphasize materialism and success, do not bring real peace, happiness, or security into their life.

Instead, life seems to lead to more pain and dissatisfaction.

"The 1st Noble Truth of Suffering"

Three out of every four people on the street are under some form of treatment for various forms of depressive disorders.

For these people, the Buddha's Noble Eightfold Path offers an opportunity to understand what is really going on in this experience of life.

It's a chance to see how things actually work and what is causing the pain and suffering that goes along with anxiety, panic attacks, obsessive-compulsive behavior, sleeplessness, and depression at all levels.

Buddhist teaching offers us a helpful personal management system that can assist us in these situations.

The teaching exemplifies a simple and contented life, in which learning acceptance of each moment leads to a life that is open, happy, and free.

The Buddha taught this method of meditation that gently leads to tranquility.

This teaching opens up an inner wisdom that is pure understanding of the true nature of everything (how things really work) by systematically uncovering a series of insights, step-by-step.

This is Tranquil Wisdom Insight Meditation (TWIM) found in the Pāli texts.

It is **Samatha and Vipassanā (serenity and insight) yoked together** just as the Buddha practiced it (sutta #149 in Majjhima Nikāya).

The path of this practice leads directly to freeing our minds of its inclinations towards lust, hatred, and delusion.

It opens the way to loving acceptance of the present moment, offering us space for responses rather than re-actions in our lives.

The practice teaches us how to have an open mind that expands beyond its present limitations, so that we can examine things with calmer and deeper understanding.

In the Kalama Sutta, the Buddha explicitly stated that one should always examine and investigate and not blindly follow any belief or practice!

His admonishment in this direction was for the purpose of opening and expanding a meditator's experience, so that they will not be attached to any particular doctrine without thorough investigation.

He was attempting to depart from a traditional Teacher/Student dictatorial relationship and create an environment in which the students took responsibility fully for their own journey of inquiry.

This kind of honest inquiry into any particular doctrine opens mind, expands consciousness, and understanding through personal experience and discovery.

The meditator learns how to see personally what leads to a closed or tight mind and what leads to a mind that is open and clear, which is a mind ready to consider peace rather than war.

Preparing the Soil

One lesson the Buddha taught is to first prepare the soil for the growth of wisdom.

The soil, called "**bumi**" in Pāli, consists of the condition of the meditator's heart capacity for conscious awareness, levels of observation skill, and ability to follow precise instructions.

The heart must be loosened, much like the soil of a garden, and prepared properly through the practice of generosity (dāna).

This kind of generosity must have no expectations of receiving anything in return.

It is a practice for all aspects of the meditator's life.

This "kingly" generosity manifests as giving through kind thoughts, kind speech, and kind actions.

A person who is miserly has a tendency to have a selfish, tight, and limited mind.

When mind's attention holds on to material things (craves them), it easily becomes attached and pre-occupied.

This kind of attention becomes very personal (Attā) and leads us to immeasurable mental and physical pain and suffering (dukkha).

This is **I/Me/Mine** attachment (Attā)!

Attachment of any form makes mind uncomfortable, tense, and tight (craving).

By encouraging the practice of generosity, the meditator learns what a joyful, open and clear mind, which is never closed or tight, actually feels like.

Another form of generosity is the giving of time and energy to help those who are having problems, i.e. to become real friends.

This includes helping others to be happy!

Saying or performing actions, which cause people to smile and become happy, opens the meditator's mind and joy arises for them too.

Having this type of experience helps the meditator to expand the mind and let go of the tension, which is caused by craving.

Each time a meditator helps another person to have joy arise and experiences it themselves also, a new sensation of openness and calmness is noticed.

So you see, this is the first step in preparing the soil (bumi) for successful meditation.

Using Precepts — Fertilizing the Soil

The Buddha also emphasized the importance of keeping one's moral disciplines (sīla) in line and it *can't be overstated* how important this is when attempting to retrain mind.

Of course these precepts are rules of morality found in almost all religious settings. In that sense, discussing the precepts could be looked upon as a talk about morality. But what if we changed this from the perspective of a lecture on morality to a perspective of how the meditator can develop mindfulness and fertilize the soil?

In that case, these precepts become advice given from a "soil preparation manual."

In reality, if the meditator doesn't keep the precepts, then efforts to harvest the fruits are without results.

This should be evident today by how many meditators are literally hitting the wall and not making progress.

In some traditions stories now show up that list excuses for why this is happening to them, along with encouragement not to give up!

Not to follow the precepts is like taking the nutrients out of the soil and still expecting it to produce a crop. It won't!

These five precepts actually release mind from fear, anxiety, guilt, and remorseful feelings, when they are continually kept and practiced.

The precepts help keep your garden free from destructive pests!

If you make a commitment to keep the precepts all the time, during your entire life, then there will be no problem with your mind garden.

As a meditator you will be ready to grow a bountiful harvest of happiness and contentment.

In some cases, you may need to clean out the weeds before planting.

The good news is that the garden can be reclaimed with patience and persistence.

These five precepts are not difficult to learn.

They are:

abstaining from killing living beings;

abstaining from taking what is not given;

abstaining from wrong sexual activities;

abstaining from telling lies, using harsh speech (cursing), gossip or slander;

and abstaining from taking drugs and alcohol, which cloud mind and lead to breaking the other four precepts.

If you follow this operational advice all during life, then your meditation will function very well.

This is how the meditator prepares the soil for planting so your mind garden will bloom.

The essence of meditation is to open and calm the mind, so that the meditator can peacefully accept whatever arises without any tightening.

Subsequently, the Buddha taught the methods of meditation (bhavana) or mental development to free mind from what restricts this understanding.

Thus, this book of instructions is written for those who are on this noble quest.

We should remember that this is a gradual teaching, resulting in gradual learning and offers many levels of accomplishment that are very useful in everyday life.

For the beginner, these instructions may appear confusing and difficult to understand at first, but you will gradually discover many benefits if followed very closely.

In actual fact, there is no evidence that meditation, as taught by the Buddha in the beginning, was broken into different types of techniques like concentration and insight, as is commonly practiced today.

In the end, the Buddha's full awakening was not reached through deep one-pointed concentration in any of its forms, that is, fixed or absorption concentration (appaṇā samādhi), access or neighborhood concentration (upacāra samādhi), or moment-to-moment concentration (khaṇikha samādhi).

These types of one-pointed concentration meditation practices actually bring tightness to mind and suppress the hindrances with a lack of deep understanding.

This type of concentration meditation is a form of suppression, a type of cutting off of one's experience, which causes a kind of resistance (craving) composed of tension and tightness. As a result, there is a conflict with reality. On the other hand, Tranquil Wisdom Insight Meditation (TWIM or samatha/vipassanā) opens the meditator's mind and continually expands it without resistance. An overly concentrated mind does not meditate in the way the Buddha practiced on the night of his awakening.

It doesn't matter whether we are talking about full, fixed, or ecstatic absorption concentration, or access concentration.

The same problem arises concerning tension and tightness.

It is most important that no matter what distracts mind's attention away from the "breath" and tranquilizing or "Loving-kindness" and relaxing, the meditator should simply recognize mind's attention moving, release, relax, re-smile, and return back to the meditation object.

Then repeat this cycle. This is called the 6R's in English, which is the practice of Right Effort (or harmonious practice) from the Noble Eight-Fold Path. The 6 R's are:

Recognize
Release
Relax
Re-Smile
Return
Repeat

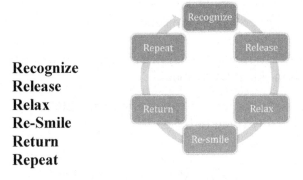

One actually let's go of the tension and tightness and tranquilizes everything without thinking about the distraction.

The actual content of arising thoughts or sensations is not important!

Seeing and understanding HOW mind's attention moves from one thing to another is the reason to meditate.

Contentment and peace arises when the meditator starts to understand the true nature of this psychophysical process that we call mind (nāma) and body (rūpa).

The meditator can learn to actually feel mind open and relax away the tension (craving)!

Next, one softly smiles and re-directs mind's attention back to the object of meditation, i.e. the "Breath" and relaxing or "Loving-Kindness" and relaxing.

The act of calming mind and relaxing the tightness in the head before coming back to the breath or mettā (loving-kindness) makes a huge difference between "Concentration Meditation" and "Tranquil Wisdom Insight Meditation" (TWIM).

A meditator who practices "Concentration Meditation" over-focuses on the object of meditation and thus they have the tendency to close or tighten the mind until there are no more distractions.

This type of "concentration" practice leads to deep absorption of mind and suppression of the hindrances so that they will not arise again until one's concentration fades away.

At that point, the meditator is attacked by the hindrances and is not able to recognize how they arise.

This is why a meditator experiences the suppression of the hindrances during a retreat or meditation session, but during life, when the concentration is not sustained anymore, the hindrances arise very strongly.

On the other hand, the meditator who practices Tranquil Wisdom Insight Meditation has the tendency to open mind, let go of craving, and allow mind's attention to become naturally calm.

In other words, the Tranquil Wisdom Insight Meditator (the TWIM) is not so caught up in daily life when hindrances arise and is able to have a more clear and balanced life without so much suffering in it.

In this way, the Tranquil Wisdom Insight Meditator (or TWIM) actually sees how this process works and becomes less attached to the hindrances.

The (TWIM) meditator does not suppress or force the mind to stay focused on just the object of meditation.

Instead, mind is always aware of what it is doing in the present moment.

The (TWIM) meditator is able to see HOW mind's attention becomes distracted and moves from one thing to another.

Whenever a distraction arises, the meditator follows the 6R's process, let's go, relaxes, smiles, and feels the expansion in the head before coming back to the breath and relaxing; or mettā and relaxing.

What is Craving? The Old Planting

A real question that everyone is supposed to know the answer to at this time is: what is craving?

How can one recognize "craving" when it arises?

The Buddha always used very specific definitions, when he gave discourses and everyone needs to become familiar with **his definitions,** which are different from our usual definitions most of the time.

The Buddhist definition of craving and how it can be seen is this:

When meditating, craving can always be seen and recognized as a tension or tightness in one's mind and body.

The easiest place to first see this tension or tightness is in one's head/brain.

Everyone has a thin membrane wrapped around the brain called the Meninges.

This membrane contracts every time any thought or feeling arises.

Noticing the tension within this contraction is how craving can be recognized and seen.

Being able to see this tightness and relax or let go of the contraction is practicing Right Effort or the 6R's.

When this is done, the meditator is able to see mind's attention become clear, and with no distracting thoughts arising, mind becomes very alert and pure.

This is what the Third Noble Truth (cessation) is all about!

The meditator smiles and brings this craving-free, pure mind back to the object of meditation.

This is how mind becomes pure and free from all craving.

Craving is also recognized as the "I like it" or "I don't like it" mind.

This is the very beginning of the false idea of a personal self (attā).

The use of the 6R's is the way to actually recognize and let go of craving.

What is Purifying Mind? New Tilling and Harvest!

It is in this way that the Third Noble Truth (cessation) the meditator actually finds the meaning of "**the purifying of mind**" in real terms.

Thus, as described in the sutta, Tranquil Wisdom Insight Meditation (TWIM or samatha/vipassanā) leads to wisdom, full awareness, sharp mindfulness, and eventually to the highest goal of attaining Nibbāna.

The in-breath, the out-breath, the relaxing of the tightness in the head and the opening and feeling of expansion of your mind and smiling is your **home base** for the breathing meditation.

This is also true for the mettā (loving-kindness) and relaxing meditation.

Whenever *mind goes away from home*, the meditator first let's go, relaxes the tightness again, feels mind expand and becomes calm; smile and then redirect mind's attention back to the object of meditation.

The meditator "**Always Comes Back Home**" regardless of what arises; i.e. whether it is a wandering thought, an emotional pain, a physical sensation, or any other distraction.

Emotional and physical disturbances are *all treated in exactly the same way* every time they arise!

This is an important thing to recognize and remember.

These distractions are actually a part of an impersonal process (anattā) and need to be seen as they really are.

This is by far the simplest meditation instruction that the Buddha ever gave! Not the easiest, but the simplest!

At the beginning of practice the meditator needs to look at what the end result is before getting too involved and spending time and effort developing it.

The question to ask is, "Is this technique leading to the best result for me?"

If a meditator wants to develop "concentration", then the absorption meditation is what they should practice.

If a meditator wants to develop understanding to let go of pain and suffering and wants to be free from the rounds of re-birth and death, the Buddha's path of Tranquil Wisdom Insight Meditation (TWIM) is the one to follow.

This is not to say that those who have been practicing another form of meditation are wasting their time.

Almost all meditation techniques have their advantages—one is not better than another. But the question is, what is the end result, and is that what the meditator is seeking?

Mixing Disciplines

It is NEVER a good idea to mix disciplines!

Mixing and matching techniques will stop the progress and whatever end result the meditator is looking for will be slow in coming or will never be accomplished.

If someone wants to make a cake and doesn't follow the precise recipe, and then add other ingredients not called for, what kind of result will come out?

It is the same with meditation!

The Buddha taught that there are many different meditation objects and how to use the Tranquil Wisdom Insight Meditation (TWIM or samatha/vipassanā) technique with each one of those objects of meditation.

But there is only one recipe to follow that leads to freedom from suffering and Nibbāna.

The Tranquil Wisdom Insight Meditation (TWIM or samatha/ vipassanā) fulfills that recipe.

The meditator never has to "control" mind's attention in a heavy, jerky, or forceful way.

Just lightly use the 6R's and this will naturally lead to a happy mind that is free from all kinds of suffering and unwholesomeness.

Attempting to push or control, and make the meditation be the way the meditator wants it to be, is the cause of more craving to arise and this is the origin of suffering.

That's it in a nutshell

The rest of the book describes these instructions, but with more precise explanations.

As you examine and explore the meanings in this book, you will begin to understand and gradually apply this technique in your meditation sittings as well as during your daily activities.

At the same time, you will **marvel** at the beauty and simplicity of the Buddha's Mindfulness of Breathing (Ānāpānasati) and Mindfulness of Loving-Kindness (Mettā) Meditations.

May all who read this book find it helpful and may they reach the highest goal.

Of Rose-Apples, Bodhis, and The Way to Nibbāna

In recent years, there have been many expositions of the Buddha's teachings in English and other languages.

However, a great number of them lack authenticity and do not accurately represent the Buddha's words.

"The 3rd Noble Truth- Cessation of Suffering"

The mixing together of Hinduism (Brahmanism), yoga, tai chi, kundalini meditation, or other disciplines which are quite different in nature, are now wrongly thought to "help" the Buddha's teachings along.

Many books are written and taught in such a free-lance way that it is difficult even to recognize them as being Buddha-Dhamma.

Thus, the purpose of these pages is to draw attention to the far- reaching significance of the Buddha-Dhamma, which includes the meditation instructions, [1] and the initial guidance to understanding his teachings and their practical applications in life.

This book attempts to give an accurate description of meditation based on the Mindfulness of Mettā Meditation and the Mindfulness of Breathing— Ānāpānasati with only limited use of standard commentaries.

The framework of the suttas used in this book are first based on the English version of the *Majjhima: Middle Length Discourses*, translated from Pāli by the Venerable Ñāṇamoli and Venerable Bhikkhu Bodhi and published by Wisdom Publications. Many other English translations have been reviewed as well in the process of building this book.

To help in meditation, many English words have been chosen by Venerable Vimalaraṁsi, so that the readers can understand more clearly how to apply this training in their practice. These words were tested with thousands of students over a fourteen-year period.

This book discusses the sutta, gives the instruction for the meditation, and shows the meditator that the basic technique for both Mindfulness of Mettā (Loving-kindness) and Mindfulness of Breathing (Ānāpānasati) **are used in the same way.**

Even though these are different objects of meditation, the meditator will find that the basic instructions given within the sutta are fulfilled by the use of the 6R's.

These 6R's fulfill the steps of Right Effort that were given to us by the Buddha.

With the Mindfulness of Mettā Meditation, the author uses some of the instructions in the commentaries before going to the instructions given in the suttas because they help Western meditators to see how to let go of old attachments quickly and easily.

These commentaries seem to agree very much with the suttas concerning this part.

Practicing the Mettā (Loving-Kindness) in this way has proven to be most helpful for serious meditators interested in developing their personality to become wholesome and happy!

We will first start by redefining some words, which are regularly misunderstood or badly used to suit some commentaries.

These misuses do cause a lot of confusion to the practice of the Buddha's method of meditation. There is a glossary of words in the back of this book that will help in clarifying the meaning.

Jhāna

First, let us look at the word *jhāna*. In Pāli, *jhāna* has many types of meanings.

It can mean "meditation stages" or "illumination." *Jhāna* can also mean "**levels of understanding.**"

However, when the common translation of the word jhāna as being merely "concentration" is used, misunderstanding takes place.

The author also observed that the word *jhāna* was never defined in the suttas as "fixed concentration" or "access concentration" or "momentary concentration."

These definitions are only mentioned in some commentaries and this incorrect definition has caused much confusion and misled the unaware meditator to wrong kinds of practice that lead away from Nibbāna.

The Buddha invariably includes the word *jhāna* (meditation stages of understanding, not fixed absorption of mind) in the full and gradual training.

According to the suttas, these meditation stages are not mystical or magical experiences that lead only to psychic powers.

They are the way to develop one's observation skills in order to see Dependent Origination and the Four Noble Truths clearly.

These meditation stages of understanding (*jhāna*) contribute to the built-in perfection of the path, which emphasizes deep tranquility, wisdom, stillness, opening of mind, collectedness, letting go of craving, and smiling.

These qualities provide a solid base for the realization of both calmness of mind, insight, and the development of wisdom (this always refers to seeing and understanding Dependent Origination in practical ways).

While they are still mundane, the *jhāna* is the very **"footsteps of the Tathāgata"** that forms the gradual training, which really does lead to Nibbāna in this very life.

The word *jhāna* (stage of understanding) is mentioned many thousands of times in the suttas and is an essential part of the liberation that leads to Nibbāna!

Samatha

Next is the Pāli word ***samatha.***

The more accurate meaning of samatha is peacefulness, calmness, tranquility, serenity, or stillness, and not as commonly translated, terms like "absorption" or "fixed concentration."

Thus, the author prefers to use the words serenity, collectedness, or tranquility.

Samādhi

The Pāli word **samādhi** is equally important!

Samādhi has many different meanings, such as collectedness, calmness, unified mind, tranquility, peacefulness, stillness, composure of mind, quiet mind, serenity, and one of the lesser meanings, "concentration."

This word *concentration* refers to a type of mental development that is different from the commonly practiced fixed absorption.

Thus, the true meaning is not merely "fixed absorption concentration or access concentration," but calmness or stillness with sharp and open awareness in different degrees.

Interestingly, Rhys-Davids the first translator of the Buddhist text into English, found through his studies, that the word *samādhi* was never used before the time of the Buddha.[2]

Even though as a Bodhisatta the Buddha did practice "absorption concentration meditation," this word has a different meaning from "concentration."

The Buddha made up and "popularized" the word *samādhi* to express collectedness, calm wisdom, tranquility, openness, smiling, and awareness, along with developing a mind, which has clarity and wisdom in it.

Later, the Brahmins changed the meaning to "absorption concentration."

Hence, the author will use either collectedness, composure of mind, or unified mind.

Anyone who chooses to use the word "concentration" must know that it means collectedness, stillness of mind, composure of mind, or a unified mind.

Not absorption, fixed (appaṇā), or access (upacāra) concentration or even momentary (Khaṇikha) concentration. Why?

Because these fixed states of concentration will suppress the hindrances, which is where our true attachments are stored.

Stopping the hindrances from arising will prevent the meditator from ever purifying the mind (citta).

The hindrances are where craving forms our attachments (Second Noble Truth—the cause of suffering is craving); therefore, if one's deep concentration suppresses them, how can the meditator ever see and let go of craving?

This book is written with a deep conviction that the systematic cultivation of Tranquil Wisdom Insight Meditation (TWIM or samatha/vipassanā) *brings both insights* into the seeing of the true nature of this psychophysical (mind/body) process and serenity of mind at the same time! This is stated often in the suttas.

Furthermore, there is the seeing and realizing the cause and effect relationships of all dependent conditions.

This means seeing the impersonal process of Dependent Origination, the Four Noble Truths, and the three characteristics of all existence (anicca, dukkha, and anattā), which is the development of penetrative wisdom.

These clear insights lead to dispassion, emancipation, and awakening.

As a matter of fact, the Buddha discovered that absorption or one-pointed types of concentration practice of any kind did not lead him to freedom from suffering or Nibbāna. But, in fact they lead away from true freedom from suffering.

After becoming a homeless one, the Bodhisatta (future Buddha) went to two different teachers of absorption concentration meditation.

His first teacher was Ālāra Kalama.

After learning the Dhamma and Discipline, he practiced until he attained a very high and distinguished stage of meditation called the "Realm of Nothingness."

The Bodhisatta (future Buddha) then went to his teacher and asked whether he could proceed any further with that meditation.

Ālāra Kalama replied that it was the highest stage anyone could attain.

The Bodhisatta (future Buddha) was dissatisfied and went to another teacher by the name of Uddaka Rāmaputta.

He learned the Dhamma and Discipline, then practiced it and attained the absorption jhāna, called the "realm of neither-perception nor non-perception."

The Bodhisatta (future Buddha) again went to his teacher and asked a similar question about there being more to attain.

Again, the Bodhisatta (future Buddha) was told that this was absolutely the highest attainment anyone could ever achieve.

The future Buddha (bodhisatta) was disappointed, because he saw that there were still many more things to let go of.

He observed that these absorption types of concentration techniques, which focused intensely on the object of meditation as if he was glued to it, caused major tightening of mind's attention.

He reasoned that there was still attachment whenever there was tension in mind (craving).

He also noticed that, if any part of the experience was suppressed or not allowed to arise, then mind was not really purified from these fetters.

Suppression occurs with every form of concentration (that is, fixed absorption concentration or access concentration)—there was still some kind of holding on or attachment to the false idea of a personal ego or self-belief (attā).

Thus, after six long years of trying all of the various spiritual and ascetic practices from body mortifications, such as starving the body, holding the breath, and crushing mind with mind, he realized that these practices did not lead him to a calm and open mind and body that was free from attachment and suffering.

On the night of the Bodhisatta's (future Buddha) realization of the supreme Nibbāna, he recalled an incident at a ploughing festival while he was just a young boy of one or two years old.

When his attendants left him alone under a rose-apple tree, he sat in "Tranquil Wisdom Insight Meditation" (samatha/vipassanā) and experienced a mind that was expanded and open, completely free from all tension or tightness (craving)!

He saw that this form of meditation would lead him to the experience of the "tranquility jhāna" (samatha/vipassanā), instead of the "concentration [absorption] jhāna." [3]

As a result of the Tranquil Wisdom Insight Meditation (TWIM or samatha/vipassanā), his mind was filled with joy; his body became light and happy.

When the joy faded away, he then experienced strong tranquility and peacefulness.

His mind and body became very comfortable and at ease.

His mind was composed, very still with sharp mindfulness and full awareness of what was happening around him, i.e., he could still hear sounds and feel sensations with his body at that time.

When the Bodhisatta (future Buddha) sat under the Bodhi tree to meditate on the full-moon night of May and made his great effort to attain the supreme Nibbāna, he recalled that not all forms of pleasure are unwholesome.

He had these thoughts because he had practiced so many austerities to make pleasant feeling go away by torturing himself.

He realized that there could be pleasurable feelings arising in mind and body, although there was not any attachment to anything.

That very night the Bodhisatta practiced Tranquil Wisdom Insight Meditation (TWIM or samatha/vipassanā) through the method of the 6R's (Right Effort).

Understanding Right Effort

The 6R's are:

Recognize - that mind is distracted.

Release - mind's attention away from those distractions. This means that the meditator allows the distraction to be there without keeping mind's attention on it. The 6R's are not a way of making distractions go away!

They are teaching the meditator to allow things to be, without "making" them be anything other than they are.

Relax - the tension or tightness caused by that distraction.

This is the **most important** part of the 6R's, because it is the letting go of craving!

Re-smile - to bring up a wholesome state of mind.

Return - mind's attention back to the breath and relaxing on the in-breath and relaxing on the out-breath or sending mettā to a spiritual friend—relaxing and smiling.

Repeat - the process of staying on the breath and relaxing

These 6R's are a way of practicing Right Effort in the Eight-Fold Path. That is:

1. **Recognizing** when mind has become distracted by an unwholesome distraction,
2. **Letting go** of that unwholesome distraction and relax,
3. **Bringing up** a wholesome object (smiling) and return back to the breath and relaxing, then
4. **Staying** on the loving-kindness and relaxing or the breath and relaxing.

These are all four of the steps to Right Effort!

More on this later in the book.

In short, the Buddha practiced the Ānāpānasati or Mindfulness of Breathing.

Later, he developed the Mindfulness of Loving-Kindness meditation.

And as we all know, he became the Buddha or the supremely enlightened one.

The Ānāpānasati Sutta, taught by the Lord Buddha 2600 years ago, still provides the most direct, simplest, thorough, and effective method for training and developing mind.

The Buddha also taught the Mindfulness of Mettā or Loving-Kindness Meditation as a tool that leads the meditator directly to the attainment of Nibbāna, even more quickly and easily than any other kind of meditation practice.

For keeping mind's attention on daily tasks and problems as well as for its highest aim—mind's own unshakable deliverance from greed, hatred, and delusion.

The method described here is taken directly from the sutta itself and its results can be seen clearly and easily when the meditator practices according to the instructions in the sutta.

The author emphasizes that the instructions in this book are not his own opinion, but is actually the Buddha's own instruction given in a clear and precise way.

This can be called the **"*Undiluted Dhamma*,"** because it comes directly from the suttas themselves, without a lot of additions or free-lance ideas.

The Ānāpānasati Sutta gives the **most** profound meditation instructions available today.

It includes the Four Foundations of Mindfulness, the Seven Awakening Factors, and The Eight-Fold Path, and shows how they are fulfilled through the practice of Mindfulness of Breathing and the Mindfulness of Metta meditations.

This is done by attaining all of the meditation stages of understanding (jhāna or Right Collectedness).[4]

This sutta shows the direct way to practice Tranquil Wisdom Insight Meditation (TWIM) and does not categorize meditation practices into separate types of meditation.

Strangely, the current separation into various types of meditation, such as "fixed absorption concentration" or "access concentration" and "momentary concentration" meditation, seems to occur only in the commentaries but never in the suttas.

Thus, it is important to notice this and compare them with the suttas for their accuracy.

From the attainment of the fourth jhāna, three alternative lines of further development become possible.

This Ānāpānasati sutta deals with only one of those, namely the attainment of all the material and immaterial jhāna (levels of understanding), followed by the experience of the "Cessation of Perception, Feeling, and Consciousness" (nirodha samapatti in Pāli) and finally the realization of the Four Noble Truths and Dependent Origination (Paṭiccasamuppāda).

In these attainments, the Buddha mentions four meditative stages that continue the mental unification established by the jhāna (levels of understanding).

These states described as "the liberation that are peaceful and immaterial," are still mundane states.

Distinguished from the material jhānas (meditation stages of understanding) by their deepening of the subtle mental observations, they are named after their own surpassed stages (so called because they go beyond the material jhāna):

"the base of infinite space, the base of infinite consciousness, the base of nothingness, the base of neither-perception nor non-perception, (neither feeling nor non-feeling, and neither consciousness nor non-consciousness)."

These bases are very attainable if meditators ardently and continually keep their daily meditation practice going.

Since this is a gradual training, meditators first must learn to walk before they can run.

Thus, the beginning of the meditation practice is the basis for further development.

This is a straight and direct path towards liberation and the Supramundane Nibbāna.

It does, however, require sustained meditative effort, applied to a simple object of meditation to watch, i.e., Mettā Meditation (Loving-kindness) and the breath, followed by the relaxation and expansion of mind which allows mind's attention to become calm and clear without distractions.

This is commonly called the "Pure Mind," because this mind has no craving in it.

When meditators practice the Ānāpānasati Sutta as a Tranquil Wisdom Insight Meditation (TWIM) or the Mindfulness of Metta—Loving-Kindness Meditation (TWIM), they find that their creativity and intuition increase as their practice develops.

This forms the timeless and universal appeal of a true Doctrine of Awakening (realizing Dependent Origination and the Four Noble Truths, while experiencing the three characteristics of all existence in each link), which has the depth and breadth, the simplicity and intelligence for providing the foundation and the framework of a living *Dhamma for All.*

One will sense the urgency of the fundamental "non-materialistic" problems and search for solutions that neither science nor the "religions of faith" can provide.

More important is the final realization, which comes through the method of Tranquil Wisdom Insight Meditation (TWIM or samatha/vipassanā) that invokes experiencing the various meditation stages of understanding (jhāna) and seeing and understanding through direct knowledge, all of the links of Dependent Arising.

This means seeing and realizing directly all of the Four Noble Truths.

The true aim of the Mettā Meditation (Mindfulness of Loving-Kindness) and the Ānāpānasati (Mindfulness of Breathing) is nothing less than final liberation from suffering, which is the highest goal of the Buddha's Teachings—Nibbāna.

The practice of the Buddhist Path evolves in two distinct stages, a mundane (lokiya) or preparatory stage and a supramundane (lokuttara) or accomplished stage.

The mundane path is developed when the disciples undertake the gradual training in developing their virtues (continually keeping the precepts), tranquility, collectedness, deep composure of mind, and developing wisdom.

This reaches its peak in the practice of Tranquil Wisdom Insight Meditation (TWIM or samatha/vipassanā) and the 6R's, which deepens direct experience.

At the same time, this shows one the three characteristics of existence, that is:

- Impermanence (anicca),
- Unsatisfactoriness (dukkha), and

- The impersonal nature of all existence (anattā).

Nibbāna

In short, there are two kinds of nibbāna: one is the worldly or mundane type of nibbāna and the other is the supramundane or unworldly type of nibbāna.

The mundane or worldly type of nibbāna is attained every time the meditator lets go of craving (taṇhā), which is an attachment or hindrance.

Relief arises along with a kind of happiness when this relax step is added.

This type of nibbāna will occur many thousands, hundreds of thousands of times, when one uses the 6R's during meditation and seriously practices Tranquil Wisdom Insight Meditation (TWIM).

*The supramundane type of nibbāna only occurs **after** the meditator sees and realizes Dependent Origination (Paṭiccasamuppāda), both arising and cessation.*

This supramundane nibbāna takes time and effort to achieve.

However, that does not mean that it is impossible for lay men and lay women to attain it.

They do so by persistent daily practice and by taking an occasional meditation retreat with a competent teacher who understands how the 6R's, Tranquil Wisdom Insight Meditation, and Dependent Origination occur.

Even those who live active lives in the world can still achieve the highest goal of the Supramundane Nibbāna.

This is mentioned during the time of the Buddha, in the Parinibbāna Sutta (MN # 73, the Mahāvocchagotta Sutta:

The Greater Discourse to Vacchagotta, of the Majjhima Nikāya, published by Wisdom Publications),

Many more lay men and lay women became saints than the monks (both male and female) when they practiced on a regular basis.

The common belief that one must be a bhikkhu or bhikkhuni in order to reach this goal is just *not true*.

The Buddha taught the four-fold Sangha, that is, bhikkhus, bhikkhunis, lay men and lay women.

The exhortation of the Lord Buddha was for all people who were interested in the correct path to **Ehipassiko** (a Pāli word meaning "come and see").

This is very good advice, because it helps those who are interested to get out of the judgmental, critical mind and honestly practice to see if this is, in fact, the right way.

Dependent Origination—the Spine of the Teaching

What makes the Buddha's path so unique amongst all other types of meditation in his revelation of the Impersonal Process of Dependent Origination which is taught within the teaching?

During his period of struggle for awakening, Dependent Origination came as a **marvelous** and eye-opening discovery that ended his pursuit in the darkness:

> *Arising, arising—thus, monks, in regard to things unheard before there arose in me vision, knowledge, wisdom, understanding and radiance. (Samyutta Nikāya X11. 65/ii.105).*

Once enlightened, the mission of the Tathāgata is to proclaim Dependent Origination (This means the Four

Noble Truths, too.) to the world (Saṃyutta Nikāya X11.25-6).

The Buddha taught this in discourse after discourse, so much so, that the Four Noble Truths and Dependent Origination have become the backbone of his teachings and is the *most essential and important* teaching of all!

While the Buddha was still only an unenlightened Bodhisatta, he worked very hard to find the way to attain liberation—Nibbāna. In the Saṃyutta Nikāya (Book IV, Book of Causation, Chapter XII, pages 537-539. Origination) he describes the way he reasoned out the arising of the links of Dependent Origination and HOW they cease. He says:

> *Monks, before my enlightenment while I was still only a Bodhisatta, not yet enlightened, it occurred to me:*
>
> *Alas, this world has fallen into trouble, in that it is born, ages, and dies, it passes away and is reborn, yet it does not understand the escape from this suffering headed by aging and death (jarā-maraṇa).*
>
> *When now will an escape be recognized from this suffering headed by aging-and-death (jarā-maraṇa)?*
>
> *Then it occurred to me: When what exists does aging-and-death (jarā-maraṇa) come to be? By what is aging-and-death (jarā-maraṇa) conditioned?*
>
> *Then through careful attention, there took place in me a breakthrough by wisdom:*

When there is birth (jāti), aging-and-death (jarā-maraṇa) comes to be; aging-and-death (jarā-maraṇa) has birth (jāti) as its condition.

Then it occurred to me: 'When what exists does birth (jāti) come to be? By what is birth (jāti) conditioned?

Then through careful attention, there took place in me a breakthrough by wisdom:

When there is existence (bhava—habitual tendency), birth (jāti) comes to be; birth has existence (bhava—habitual tendency) as its condition."

Then it occurred to me: 'When what exists does existence (bhava—habitual tendency) come to be? By what is existence (bhava - habitual tendency) conditioned?

Then through careful attention, there took place in me a breakthrough by wisdom:

When there is clinging, existence (bhava—habitual tendency) comes to be; existence (bhava—habitual tendency) has clinging as its condition.

Then it occurred to me: When what exists does clinging (upādāna) come to be? By what is clinging (upādāna) conditioned?

Then through careful attention, there took place in me a breakthrough by wisdom:

When there is craving (taṇhā), clinging (upādāna) comes to be; clinging (upādāna) has craving (taṇhā) as its condition.

Then it occurred to me: When what exists does craving (taṇhā) come to be? By what is craving (taṇhā) conditioned?

Then through careful attention, there took place in me a breakthrough by wisdom:

When there is feeling (vedanā), craving (taṇhā) comes to be; craving (taṇhā) has feeling (vedanā) as its condition.

Then it occurred to me: When what exists does feeling (vedanā) come to be? By what is feeling (vedanā) conditioned?

Then through careful attention, there took place in me a breakthrough by wisdom:

When there is contact (phassa), feeling (vedanā) comes to be; feeling (vedanā) has contact (phassa) as its condition.

Then it occurred to me: When what exists does contact (phassa) come to be? By what is contact (phassa) conditioned?

Then through careful attention, there took place in me a breakthrough by wisdom:

When there is the six sense bases (saḷāyatana), contact (phassa) comes to be; contact (phassa) has the six sense bases (saḷāyatana) as its condition.

Then it occurred to me: When what exists do the six sense bases (saḷāyatana) come to be? By what are the six sense bases (saḷāyatana) conditioned?

Then through careful attention there took place in me a breakthrough by wisdom:

When there are mentality/materiality (nāma-rūpa), the six sense bases (saḷāyatana) come to be; The six sense bases (saḷāyatana) have mentality/materiality (nāma-rūpa) as their condition.

Then it occurred to me: When what exists do mentality/materiality (nāma-rūpa) come to be? By what are mentality/materiality (nāma-rūpa) conditioned?

Then through careful attention there took place in me a breakthrough by wisdom:

When there is consciousness (viññāṇa), the mentality/materiality (nāma-rūpa) come to be; Mentality/materiality (nāma-rūpa) has consciousness (viññāṇa) as their condition.

Then it occurred to me: 'When what exists does consciousness (viññāṇa) come to be? By what is consciousness (viññāṇa), conditioned?

Then through careful attention there took place in me a breakthrough by wisdom:

When there are formations (saṅkhāra), consciousness (viññāṇa) comes to be;

consciousness (viññaṇa) has formations (saṅkhāra) as its condition.

Then it occurred to me: When what exists do formations (saṅkhāra) come to be? By what are formations (saṅkhāra), conditioned?

Then through careful attention there took place in me a breakthrough by wisdom:

When there is ignorance (avijjā), formations (saṅkhāra) come to be; formations (saṅkhārā) have ignorance (avijjā) as its condition.

Thus with ignorance (avijjā) as condition formations (saṅkhāra) come to be;

with formations (saṅkhāra) as condition consciousness (viññaṇa) comes to be;

with consciousness (viññaṇa) as condition mentality/materiality (nāma-rūpa) comes to be;

with mentality/materiality (nāma-rūpa) as condition the six sense bases (saḷāyatana) come to be;

with the six sense bases (saḷāyatana) as condition contact (phassa) comes to be;

with contact (phassa) as condition feeling (vedanā) comes to be;

with feeling (vedanā) as condition craving (taṇhā) comes to be;

*with craving (taṇhā) as condition clinging
(upādāna) comes to be;*

*with clinging (upādāna) as condition existence
(bhava—habitual tendency) comes to be;*

*with existence (bhava—habitual tendency) as
condition birth (Jāti) comes to be;*

*with birth (Jāti) as condition aging and death
(jarā-maraṇa), sorrow, lamentation, pain,
grief, and despair come to be.*

Such is this whole mass of suffering.

*"Origination, origination"—thus monks, in
regard to things unheard before there arose
in me vision, knowledge, wisdom, true
knowledge, and radiance.*

Then in the next sutta on page 539 of the same book the
Buddha talks about how he discovered the way leading to
the cessation of these links: it says,

*Then it occurred to me: When what does not
exist does aging-and-death come not to be?*

*With the cessation of what does aging-and-
death not come to be?*

*Then through careful attention, there took
place a breakthrough by wisdom:*

*When there is no birth, aging-and-death does
not come to be; with the cessation of birth,
comes the cessation of aging-and-death.*

Dependent Origination

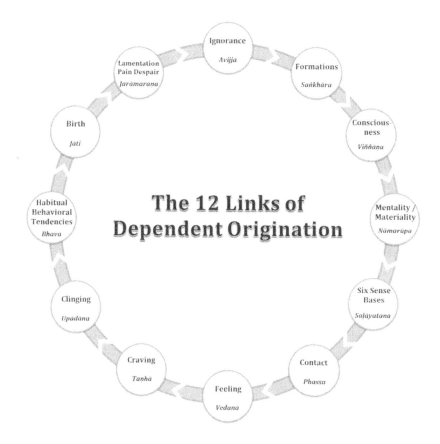

The 12 Links of Dependent Origination

- Ignorance — *Avijjā*
- Formations — *Saṅkhāra*
- Consciousness — *Viññāna*
- Mentality / Materiality — *Nāmarūpa*
- Six Sense Bases — *Saḷāyatana*
- Contact — *Phassa*
- Feeling — *Vedanā*
- Craving — *Taṇhā*
- Clinging — *Upādāna*
- Habitual Behavioral Tendencies — *Bhava*
- Birth — *Jāti*
- Lamentation Pain Despair — *Jarāmarana*

It then goes all of the way through the cessation of these links, even though this is the most important aspect of the teaching, i.e. learning how to have the suffering cease.

The author will allow the reader to do some research on his or her own and read the rest of this sutta from the texts for themselves. The next sutta, p. 539, is talking about the cessation of all of these links and the author won't go through them all again, here.

The reason that this sutta on the Origination of suffering was put in its entirety is to show that as a *bodhisatta*, the future Buddha had this formula worked out before the night of his Awakening.

This impersonal process of Dependent Origination and the Four Noble Truths was never known before the *bodhisatta* figured it out.

Teaching the Right Way and the Wrong Way

There is one more thing about the teachings of the Buddha that needs to be mentioned. The Buddha stated in the preceding sutta (page 536, The Two Ways) that there are two ways to teach the Dhamma. The wrong way and the right way!

The wrong way is by teaching only suffering. Many teachers these days tell their students that the Buddha taught that everything is suffering, all life is suffering!

And according to the Buddha this is the wrong way to teach.

The Buddha said that the right way to teach is teaching about the Cessation of Suffering and how this leads to liberation (the Third Noble Truth).

The emphasis on saying that "everything in life is a form of suffering" is very disturbing to many people, especially beginners, and with good reason!

This is why some people say that Buddhism is a pessimistic religion.

In fact, it is a very optimistic way of looking at life!

To have a life with the answers to overcoming suffering of course is the most important insight.

When a teacher focuses on the Cessation of Suffering and that it can be attained in this very life, the gloom of suffering and pain lifts, then it is replaced with happiness, contentment, and smiles!

When the Venerable Arahat Assaji was asked to state the Master's message as precisely and as briefly as possible, he gave the doctrine of arising and ceasing of phenomena as seen through the eyes of Dependent Origination.

With a single sentence, the Lord Buddha dispels doubt about the correctness of this summary: *"He who sees Dependent Origination sees the Dhamma, he who sees the Dhamma sees Dependent Origination."* (Middle Length Sayings [Majjhima Nikāya], Sutta 28 Section 38, published by Wisdom Publications).

This means seeing and realizing all of the Noble Truths along with the links of Dependent Origination and the three characteristics.

This is the only way to attain Nibbāna!

When one's faculties have gained a degree of maturity and they see the links of Dependent Origination clearly, the mundane path rises to the supramundane path, because it leads directly and surely out of Suffering.

One then realizes The Origin of Suffering, The Cessation of Suffering, and The Path Leading the Way Out of Suffering.

There is another interesting sutta about seeing the Four Noble Truths, found in the Digha Nikāya Sutta number 16, Section 5.27.

From this section of the sutta, one concludes that the way to attain awakening is by following the Eightfold Path and realizing the Noble Truths. It says:

5.27 In whatever Dhamma and Discipline the Noble Eightfold Path is not found, no ascetic is found of the first grade (meaning a Sotāpanna), second grade (meaning Sakadāgāmī), third grade (meaning Anāgāmī), or fourth grade (meaning an Arahat). But such ascetics can be found, of the first, second, third, and fourth grade in a Dhamma and Discipline where the Noble Eightfold Path is found. Now, Subhadda, in this Dhamma and Discipline the Noble Eightfold Path is found, and in it are to be found ascetics of the first, second, third and fourth grade. Those other schools are devoid of [true] ascetics; but if in this one the monks were to live to perfection, the world would not lack for Arahats.

Mind opens when it sees and realizes the insight into the links of Dependent Origination directly.

This is such a big and deep insight that the author has begun calling it the true "Oh, WOW!" experience.

Practical Application of the Eight-Fold Path

There are actually many different ways and levels to talk about the Eight-Fold Path, which is the most important facet of the Buddha's Teachings, when seen in Dependent Origination.

In relationship to the development of Meditation, the way we need to discuss this is through the applied aspects of doing the meditation and using a much deeper, but still a very practical approach to understanding how the Eight-Fold Path works.

The normal ways of thinking about the Eight-Fold Path are:

1. Right View
2. Right Thought
3. Right Speech
4. Right Action
5. Right Livelihood
6. Right Effort
7. Right Mindfulness
8. Right Concentration

"The 4th Noble Truth" The Path

They are commonly put into the three categories of Morality (Sīla), Concentration (Samādhi), and Wisdom (Paññā)

But actually all of this is only the surface way of looking at this.

The explanation here about this path is a much deeper way that relates directly to meditation and to the meditator's training of how to do observations of Dependent Origination.

In order to present a slightly different way of looking at this, things have been changed a bit, so that it will become easier to understand.

The reason is that, when this Path is broken into three categories, the middle category (sīla) is most often forgotten about.

This is because morality (sīla), when looked at this way, doesn't really seem to have anything to do with the meditation practice.

Dividing up the Eight-Fold Path can effectively change it to a Five-Fold Path.

This kind of surface interpretation doesn't tend to help or deepen one's own personal investigation and understanding of the Dhamma.

When the changes in both words and meaning are shown and explained, this will become clearer.

This Eight-Fold Path is so important that the Buddha included it in the very first discourse that he gave, The Dhammacakkappattana Sutta (The Turning of the Wheel of Dhamma).

He was teaching the first five ascetics about the correct way to practice meditation, and was showing how his understanding of the Dhamma was different from other teachings.

As it says in many suttas, *"The Dhamma is well expounded by the Buddha, it is immediately effective, and invites one to come and see, which leads to final liberation here and now."*

What this shows is that the Path to the Cessation of Suffering is an experience that can still happen today when a meditator goes back to closely practice the foundation teachings of the Buddha.

This wonderful Path to the Cessation of Suffering has eight parts and they must all be practiced at the same time while the meditator is doing the meditation.

Every fold in the Eight-Fold Path has a practical aspect to it and teaches understanding of how to let go of the suffering talked about in the Noble Truths.

Let us take a look at the Eight-Fold Path in a slightly different way.

For one thing the word *Right* seems to be a little hard for our purpose of understanding.

The author chooses to use the word "Harmonious" instead of "Right."

This tends to put a softer approach to the actual practice of meditation.

Using the word "Right" automatically brings to mind the opposite, which is "Wrong"!

This tends to make one's mind see things in black or white and nothing in between.

The word "Harmonious" doesn't seem to do this and it gives a more fluid kind of feeling to all of these different aspects of the Eight-Fold Path.

Truth seekers, as they live their lives, can ask: "Am I really being in harmony with what is happening in the present moment right now?"

This kind of question can help the meditator to remember to stay on the Path that leads to the cessation of all suffering (The Eight-Fold Path).

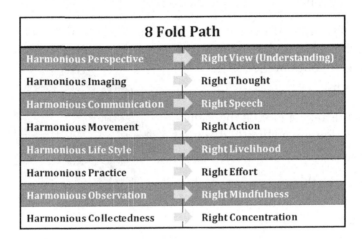

1. Sammā Diṭṭhi — Harmonious Perspective (Right View)

This is at the beginning of the Eight-Fold Path because it sets the tone of the impersonal aspects of the entire Path.

This **Harmonious Perspective** (Right View) is talking about the perspective of everything that arises as being an impersonal process (anattā) to be observed.

When out of harmony with the present moment (Dhamma or Truth), the meditator is taking whatever arises personally (attā), and then there is the personal desire to control all thoughts and sensations when they arise.

This is where the craving begins to arise, and craving always shows itself as being a tightness or tension in both mind and body. Please remember that the tightness or tension in one's head is a part of the body and needs to be relaxed also.

There is a membrane wrapped around the brain and this membrane contracts or tightens whenever a thought, feeling, or sensation arises.

This tightness is commonly called craving and is the "I like it" or "I don't like it" mind.

At that time, the meditator tries to make these phenomena be the way we want them to be.

Anytime a meditator tries to fight or control the Dhamma (Truth) of the present moment,

anytime one tries to change the Dhamma (Truth) of the present moment,

anytime one tries to make the Dhamma (Truth) of the present moment be any way other than it actually is,

this is the cause of great pain and suffering!

This is the First Noble Truth, Suffering or being out of harmony with our perspective of the present moment, when we are taking everything that arises as being part of an I/Me/Mine (attā) perspective.

Why does suffering occur?

Because of the unharmonious perspective of "I want' things to be, the way I want them to be, when I want them this way!"

This I/Me/Mine concept or perspective (attā) is the very problem to be seen, let go of, and relaxed—in all movements or shifts of mind's attention from one thing to another.

As the meditator begins to understand that all phenomena (Mentality/ Materiality, nāma-rūpa) that arise (anicca) are a part of an impersonal (anattā) process to be observed, let go of, relaxed, and smiled into,

then the meditator will be more able to see the slight tight nesses or tensions (or movement of mind's attention) caused by taking things personally.

The relaxing, when the meditator is doing the breath meditation, brings recognition of the tightness and tension. This tightness is how one recognizes all six kinds of craving (taṇhā, the craving at each sense door).

This is where the very first part of the **unharmonious perspective** (wrong view) or being out of harmony with the true nature of the impersonal perspective in all movements, and even vibrations that arise in mind's attention moment-to-moment, occurs.

When the meditator develops a **Harmonious Perspective** (right view) they let go of this kind of personal attitude, by seeing through the eyes of the impersonal nature of everything that arises in the present moment.

When the meditator takes anything as being I/Me/Mine personally, at that time, the meditator is not able to see or understand any of the Noble Truths.

Why? Because the craving (I like it…I don't like it, mind) and clinging (the stories that go along with the opinions, concepts, and the false idea of a personal self, papañca) have clouded our perspective.

This is the way mind pushes us around and makes us think that every "problem" that arises through our daily lives is an emergency and such a big problem that it seems insurmountable.

This deluded mind brings up all kinds of dissatisfaction and even depression.

If one can't see exactly how mind works, the way modern society works these days, whatever arises will be taken as being "mine" personally.

This causes a lot of suffering because the meditator struggles with "I want to control this feeling with my thoughts" and, when this approach doesn't work, out of total frustration they turn to taking drugs and/or alcohol to get relief from this pain and suffering.

This happens instead of looking at the deeper aspects of HOW mind's attention occurs and how one can actually change one's perspective from "I am this" (the false personal belief) to "It's only this" (the impersonal observation which is easy to let go of and relax).

The first step of the Eight-Fold Path is really the key that unlocks the suffering!

This step shows us the deep realization that everything that arises is simply a part of an impersonal process which can be seen most clearly through the letting go of craving (by relaxing) and seeing all movements or shifts of mind's attention as being a part of the Dukkha!

The rest of this path shows us how to do this, also.

2. Sammā Saṅkappa — Harmonious Imaging (or Right Thought):

This is the part of mind that works in images.

These images can be thoughts, feelings, concepts, or pictures.

Harmonious Imaging (Right Thought) is the consciously taking of an idea or feeling then making it recognizable and easily translated by mind.

For example, when a meditator is practicing Loving-Kindness Meditation, the instructions are to bring up a feeling of happiness, joy, calmness, etc., and feel that image.

This is consciously replacing an **unwholesome image** (wrong thought), such as fear, anxiety, depression, sadness, etc. that is currently present.

Then the meditator substitutes that unwholesome image (wrong thought) with a wholesome image like happiness, joy, peace, calmness, total acceptance, smiling, or any other uplifting image that one can think of.

Now one is purposefully feeling that wholesome, uplifting image.

If the meditator consciously brings up a wholesome thought or image like happiness or joy - they are training themselves to develop **Harmonious Imaging** (Right Thought).

In the Majjhima Nikāya Sutta # 19 Dvedhavitaka Sutta— Two Kinds of Thought, it says:

> **Whatever one frequently thinks and ponders on, this is the inclination of their mind!**

It is necessary to develop the skill of consciously manifesting a wholesome image of happiness and peace in one form or another, so that happiness, joy, and relief will be present in all of our activities.

When the meditator is practicing the breathing and relaxing meditation, any distraction that pulls attention away from the object of meditation, such as lust, aversion, restlessness, and doubt, is considered to be a type of **unwholesome image**.

The letting go of that **unharmonious image** (wrong thought) and relaxing, then redirecting mind back to the breath and relaxing is considered to be developing **Harmonious Imaging** (Right Thought) with a wholesome object of meditation.

Why? It is because they are seen and acted on, in an impersonal way (**Harmonious Perspective**—Right View, Anattā).

On the other hand, if the meditator unconsciously has the image of dissatisfaction, sadness, anxiety, frustration, worry, criticism, pride, fear, or anger etc. they are indulging in **Unharmonious Imaging** (wrong thought) which leads to suffering and pain.

Being out of harmony with an image that the meditator holds onto causes the desire to control and to fight with what is in the present moment.

This pulls us away from the present moment and the meditator begins to think of all of the reasons that they don't like that image.

This is how craving and clinging to the false idea of a self or attā identification (**unharmonious perspective**) arises.

These images lead to lots of suffering and dissatisfaction in the present moment.

As stated earlier, anytime the meditator takes an unwholesome image of what arises in the present moment to be I/Me/Mine personally, they will try to control it, fight with it, and force the present moment to be anything other than it is and this is the cause of pain and dissatisfaction (dukkha).

When a meditator notices this habit of indulging in **unharmonious images** (wrong thought—feelings, opinions, concepts, emotions that are identified with as being mine personally—attā) and they are able to gently relax and let go of that image and then softly replace it with a **harmonious image** (right thought), they are following the path that leads to the Cessation of Suffering.

Again, this can be a way of thinking, feeling, or conceptual opinions.

Letting go of those things that we take personally, then relaxing and substituting them with an uplifting image leads a person to a clear perspective (**Harmonious Perspective**) of how mind works—it is being in harmony with the present moment that has no suffering in it.

This is how the first two parts of the Eight-Fold Path interact with each other.

3. Sammā Vācā — Harmonious Communication (Right Speech):

This has to do with the gentle communication with ourselves (internal dialogue) as well as with other people.

This helps us to easily let go of and relax into any type of disturbing thoughts, feelings, or emotions that can pull mind's attention away from the meditation object (which for practical purposes we can say is the breath, relaxing and smiling, or mettā, relaxing, and smiling).

Any kind of self-criticism, or any kind of anger, dislike, worry, anxiety, dissatisfaction, condemnation, or a want to "make things be the way I want them to be" in our communication with ourselves (our internal dialogue) is a form of suffering.

For example, anger with oneself, criticism with oneself (dislike of our own actions and thoughts) and others is being out of harmony (Wrong Speech) with the present moment.

This leads to a personal belief that all thoughts, opinions, and concepts are I/Me/Mine (attā—wrong view) which leads to excessive clinging or thinking about and identifying with those thoughts.

Being out of harmony with the communication we have with ourselves, leads us to having a hard mind towards ourselves and everyone around us.

This definitely leads us to being out of harmony with any external communication with other people.

The practice of mental development is learning how to lovingly accept whatever arises in the present moment and communicating this acceptance to others and ourselves.

Or we could say that one of the things we need to practice is loving the person we are with and speaking with that love.

With whom do we spend most of our time?

That's right! We spend more time with ourselves than we do with any other person, so we really need to practice being loving and kind to ourselves as much as possible.

The Buddha said,

> *Anyone who truly loves themselves will never harm another person. (Dhammapada)*

This is how we can carry a smile around with us all of the time.

So, please smile and be happy and then cultivate those thoughts and communicate this happiness with yourself internally as well as externally to other people!

Especially, develop clear love and acceptance of ourselves about ourselves.

4. Sammā Kammanta — Harmonious Movement (Right Action):

This is very important when one is learning how to meditate!

Seeing the movements of how mind's attention goes from one thing to another is what meditation is all about!

Why? Because when meditators train their observation powers (right mindfulness), they begin to see clearly exactly how mind's attention goes from being on the breath and relaxing to a sound, sight, taste, smell, touch, or thought.

This is clearly observing exactly how the movement of mind's attention is seeing the process of Dependent Origination and how it occurs.

Being in harmony with this is the way of seeing the impersonal nature of all of these slight movements and processes.

The more interest the meditator puts into watching how mind's attention occurs, the more precise one's understanding becomes.

This observation of how mind's attention works is especially helpful in letting go, relaxing, and smiling, when the meditator has a hindrance (Nīvaraṇa) arise.

When a meditator doesn't like or see the way mind moves and then tries to control this movement, they are

experiencing unharmonious movement (or wrong action).

For instance, when a hindrance (nīvaraṇa) arises, such as restlessness, if the meditator tries to push the hindrance away or to stop the hindrance from being in the present moment, they are trying to stop mind's movements from the way they naturally occur and this is **Unharmonious Movement** (wrong action) within the practice of life.

If a meditator tries to stop or suppress mind's natural movements in such a way, the force of that concentration will temporarily stop mind's attention from moving, but, this is ONLY for a short period of time.

This includes moment-to-moment concentration (Khaṇikha Samādhi), access concentration (Upacara Samadhi), and full absorption or ecstatic concentration (Appaṇā Samādhi); all of these types of concentration are considered to be different forms of one-pointed concentration.

But, when the one-pointed concentration meditator loses strong concentration, then the movements of mind's attention tend to become stronger again and the meditator is then attacked by the hindrances (nīvaraṇa).

After returning to the object of meditation, the meditator brings back craving along with mind's attention.

This is a cause of suffering.

This is how **unharmonious perspectives** (Wrong View), **unharmonious images** (Wrong Thoughts), and **unharmonious communications** (Wrong Speech) in one's daily activities arise, which can cause huge amounts of dissatisfaction (Dukkha).

This is where true self-responsibility for our own actions can really be seen!

Seeing exactly how mind's attention moves from one object to another takes interest and precision.

Watching these slight movements of mind's attention is the thing that makes meditation so incredibly interesting and fun to observe.

5. Sammā Ājīva — Harmonious Lifestyle (or Right Livelihood):

This has always been a curious part of the Eight-Fold Path.

The standard way of describing this has been not to kill living beings on purpose, not to sell poisons or weapons, and not to deal in slavery and selling human beings.

But how does this relate directly to one's meditation practice?

If it is important enough to be put in the Eight-Fold Path, then there must be more to it that leads to the Cessation of Suffering (the Third Noble Truth).

Don't you agree?

These things do give us this idea of Right Livelihood (**Harmonious Lifestyle**) in a general way, but just how does **Harmonious Lifestyle** (Right Livelihood) relate to our true understanding and practice of meditation?

An interesting question, isn't it?

It becomes even more interesting when we consider that the Buddha gave these instructions with the very first discourse that he gave to the Five Ascetics, as he was showing them about the direct experience of meditation practice.

These ascetics surely did not kill living beings, they didn't sell poisons or weapons, or sell slaves, so what was the

Buddha actually talking about when he mentioned **Harmonious Lifestyle** (Right Livelihood)?

When we take a look at mental development through the eyes of **Harmonious Lifestyle** (Right Livelihood), it may make a little more sense.

For instance, **Harmonious Lifestyle** (Right Livelihood) means how we practice our observation (**Harmonious Observation**—Right Mindfulness) and meditation of the present moment during all of the times that we are not doing our sitting meditation (in other words, in our daily activities).

We are practicing being in harmony with a mind that is alert, calm, joyful, and uplifted (**Harmonious Movement and Harmonious Communication** or Right Action and Right speech with ourselves).

This is why the author encourages students to smile whether doing their sitting meditation or their daily activities.

The trick is seeing how, when things are not going the "way I want them to" and mind becomes heavy with emotional issues **(Unharmonious Movement** or wrong action)— how the observation of how mind's attention becomes weak and the subtle "I like it, I don't like it" and thinking unwholesome thoughts (craving and clinging— **unharmonious communication** or wrong speech) causes us even more suffering.

In other words, having a **Harmonious Lifestyle** (Right Livelihood) means that we learn to carry the meditation (**Harmonious Observation, Harmonious Communication, Harmonious Imaging, Harmonious Perspective, Harmonious Practice, Harmonious Collectedness and Harmonious Movement** in other words the entire Eight-Fold Path) with us all of the time, in our daily activities.

In this way, we then truly begin to understand that the impersonal process of Dependent Origination (**Harmonious Perspective)** is in everything that arises.

Having a **Harmonious Lifestyle** (Right Livelihood) is having an uplifted happy mind that is smiling, joyful, alert and free from unwholesome thoughts or emotions.

Emotions that are heavy and tend to pull mind away from the present moment are the cause of suffering. Why? Because the meditator tends to take these thoughts and feelings personally, with the wrong perspective of "I am that" attitude.

This personal perspective (wrong life style) in our daily lives is the reason that so many people suffer so much!

Also, too many times when someone does a meditation retreat, the meditator gets very serious and heavy in mind without really recognizing it.

The heavy distracted **Unharmonious Lifestyle** (wrong Livelihood) is the mind that is being caught by the personal (attā) belief (**Unharmonious Perspective**).

The meditator becomes distracted by opinions, concepts, thoughts, daydreaming, and the general dissatisfactions of life when the unharmonious lifestyle is present.

The way this happens is a person has a painful feeling arise.

The next thing that arises is the "'I' don't like it" mind (craving).

After this the thinking, opinions, and concepts arise and this is the internal verbalization about why "'I' don't like this" (clinging).

Then the old habitual tendency of always trying to "think" the feeling away arises.

This is HOW people cause so much pain and suffering to themselves.

The more the person tries to control the feeling with thoughts, the bigger and more intense the feeling becomes, until that person seeks some form of relief by taking drugs or alcohol.

What is a person supposed to do with that kind of situation?

It is actually rather simple!

Recognize that this situation is taking place.

Release the thoughts about how one doesn't like this feeling.

Relax the tightness caused by this distraction.

Re-smile and bring up a wholesome mind.

Return to this smile often.

Repeat this process as often as mind's attention is distracted by it.

That's it! Use these 6 steps! 6R's in English!

Notice the tight mental fist wrapped around that painful feeling.

This is aversion or the "I don't like it, "I don't want this feeling to be there" mind!

Now the question to ask yourself is:

"Did I ask this painful feeling to arise; did I say to myself I haven't had a painful feeling for a while?"

"Why don't I bring one up?"

Of course, no one is going to purposefully cause themselves pain or suffering, right?

This painful feeling arose by itself! It is an impersonal process that is occurring.

What we do with what arises in the present moment dictates what will happen in the future!

This is Karma, so the meditator has a choice:

Either try and think the feeling away, as people always do and this causes more and more suffering.

This is the old habitual way (bhava) of "handling" the situation.

OR, the meditator can try a different way of handling this.

When meditators use the 6R's, they will come to see that this painful feeling is actually a concept.

A concept is made up of lots of little parts that when they come together make up the idea of pain, for example.

If asked to show someone an automobile, what will you say to them?

Is the windshield an automobile?

Is the bumper an automobile?

Is the steering wheel an automobile?

Are the wheels an automobile?

Is the motor an automobile?

An automobile is a concept that is made up of a lot of different parts.

Pain is also a concept made up of lots of different parts and those parts are called Dependent Origination!

There is in this instance a painful **feeling (vedanā)** arising and right after that **craving (taṇhā)** arises (the I like it; I don't like it mind);

then **clinging (upādāna)** arises (the thoughts, opinions, concepts or stories about why one likes or dislikes that feeling);

then **habitual tendency (bhava)** arises (the old way of seeing and re-acting to these thoughts and feelings);

then **birth of action (Jāti)** arises;

then **sorrow, lamentation, pain, grief, and despair (jarā-maraṇa)** arise;

and this is what the Buddha called **"this whole mass of suffering."**

By using the 6R's the meditator will eventually let go of all suffering!

A human being is basically made up of five things called aggregates. They are Body (rūpa), feeling (vedanā), perception (saññā), formations or thoughts (saṅkhāra), and consciousness (viññaṇa).

Body here basically means the physical body running from top of the head down to the toes.

Feeling is pleasant, painful, or neither painful nor pleasant (not the same as emotion).

Perception is the part of mind that names things and it has memory with it also.

Formations are all of our thoughts, opinions, concepts and the strong belief in a personal self.

Consciousness is awareness of the other 4 aggregates.

Feeling is one thing and Thoughts are something else and never the two shall meet.

When a meditator tries to control a feeling with thoughts it only makes the feeling get bigger and more intense!

When using the 6R's the meditator allows the space for the feeling to be there, without getting caught by the thinking about it.

The 6R's are a tool to let the feeling be there by itself without trying to control it, no matter whether it is painful or pleasant.

The 6R's allow the space for the feeling to be there and the meditator relaxes the tightness caused by the arising of the tension or distraction, then smiles and redirects the mind's attention back to a wholesome object, that is smiling and the object of meditation.

In this way the meditator is practicing **Harmonious Lifestyle.**

Why? Because the meditator is learning how this process of Dependent Origination actually works and they are letting go of craving thereby experiencing the Third Noble Truth—the Cessation of Suffering!

Or we can say that whenever mind has heavy emotional states in it, this is considered to be **Unharmonious Lifestyle** (Wrong Livelihood).

This is a mind that is out of balance and gravitates toward unhappiness and suffering in daily activities

When one is practicing the **Harmonious Lifestyle** (Right Livelihood) it makes all meditation and life a continuous flow of happiness that leads us toward the Cessation of Suffering.

In this way, **Meditation is Life; Life is Meditation!**

6. Sammā Vāyāma — Harmonious Practice (Right Effort):

Now we come to another aspect of the Eight-Fold Path that is quite important. One of the best descriptions of **Harmonious Practice** (Right Effort) is:

When a person recognizes that the mind's attention has become distracted by a thought, feeling, or sensation, this is the first part of **Harmonious Practice** (Right Effort).

In other words, the meditator notices when an unwholesome distraction arises.

An unwholesome state is any kind of distraction that pulls mind's attention away from the object of meditation and smiling, causing mind's attention to get involved with it. i.e., taking thoughts or feelings personally (attā).

Next the meditator lets go of the distraction and relaxes the tightness or tension in both mind and body.

In other words, the meditator lets go of that unwholesome distraction by not keeping mind's attention on it and relaxes the tightness or tension in body and mind that is caused by that distraction.

These distractions can be any of the hindrances (nīrvana) and when indulged they can stop the meditator from attaining full awareness (sampajjana).

Anytime a meditator gets distracted and becomes involved with the drama they are not truly being in the present moment.

As stated earlier the hindrances (nīvaraṇa) are not to be fought with or pushed away.

Why? Because getting involved with the drama of the hindrances makes them bigger, more intense and harder to let go of.

Every time meditators try to control their thoughts or feelings, they are identifying personally (attā) with it and this causes more pain and frustration.

PLEASE don't fight with any hindrance!

Instead, learn from it.

See HOW mind's attention actually gets pulled to that hindrance; it will teach you firsthand HOW Dependent Origination occurs.

Fighting or trying to control a hindrance is the cause of the tightness or tension (craving) arising.

This happens every time mind's attention gets pulled away and this causes craving (taṇhā), clinging (upādāna), and our habitual tendency (bhava) to arise.

These are three very important parts of Dependent Origination to be recognized and observed closely. The Habitual Tendency (bhava) always re-acts in the same way when this sort of distraction arises.

The more one sees clearly how these different aspects of Dependent Origination occur the easier it is to let them go.

This is a part of the way that leads to the Cessation of Suffering!

The letting go or letting be, relaxing, and smiling is the second part of the **Harmonious Practice** (Right Effort).

The term letting go means that the person no longer keeps mind's attention on that distraction, so to be even more precise we can say; letting the distraction be there without giving it any more of mind's attention.

Next, the person gently redirects mind's smiling attention back to the object of meditation (the Breath and relaxing or Metta and relaxing), This is the third part of **Harmonious Practice** (Right Effort).

In other words, bring up a wholesome object, and this means smiling, and the meditation object; this is the third part of **Harmonious Practice** (Right Effort).

Then the person stays on the meditation object and smiles for as long as they can, naturally.

In other words, the meditator relaxes and lightly stays with the meditation object.

The key word here is "lightly."

Don't use a death grip to stay with the breath and relaxing or mettā and relaxing.

The **Harmonious Practice** is not a way to shield or block the hindrance from re-arising.

It will come up again and again, so the meditator uses this as an opportunity to learn.

Eventually the hindrance will fade away and the meditator will like what comes next. Promise!

Once again, there is a very effective way of remembering how to do this practice—it is called the 6R's:

To **RECOGNIZE** – that mind has become distracted away from the object of meditation;

To **RELEASE** - or let go of, or let the distraction be, without keeping mind's attention on it;

To **RELAX** - the tightness or tension caused by that distraction; this means to let go of the craving caused by that distraction;

To **RE-SMILE** - to bring a light mind that is very alert and calm to the meditation object;

To **RETURN** - mind's joyful attention back to the meditation object (the breath and relaxing or mettā and relaxing);

To **REPEAT** - the task of staying with the meditation object, relaxing, and smiling.

These are the 6 steps.

The smile is actually a very good tool to help mind stay uplifted and with the awakening factor of joy in one's mind, every movement of mind's attention is seen very quickly and clearly.

That is to:
RECOGNIZE
RELEASE
RELAX
RE-SMILE
RETURN
REPEAT

These words do not have to be said internally to oneself.

The meditator needs to "roll their R's" so it becomes a flowing action of allowing whatever arises to be there by itself.

The 6R's are just a reminder to let go of any distraction that pulls mind's attention away from the object of meditation.

They also help us to come back to the meditation object with a happy, clear mind that has no craving or clinging in it.

In other words, by letting go of craving and clinging and any idea you may have of a personal self is how to purify mind of all kinds of troubles, cravings, and fetters.

7. Sammā Sati — Harmonious Observation (Right Mindfulness):

This part of the Eight-Fold Path has been spoken about in very general terms.

However, the definition of Mindfulness (Sati) has never been very clear!

This is one of those words that everyone is supposed to know the definition of, but few people actually do.

Many teachers today will give the definition of Mindfulness by saying, "Just be mindful."

Another definition that has been used is to "remember, to remember, to remember," which sounds great but has very little meaning.

Now what is all of this supposed to mean?

We really need to understand that this important word must have a clear and understandable definition.

Here is a working definition that works all of the time in every situation.

Harmonious Observation (Right Mindfulness) means:

"To remember to recognize any distraction that pulls one's attention away from their object of meditation (or

whatever task you are doing in life), in the present moment."

This means to remember to observe whatever arises in the present moment, let it be, and to see the impersonal nature in all of these phenomena (**Harmonious Perspective—** Right View—anattā).

This is remembering to clearly observe how mind's attention moves (**Harmonious Movement**) from one thing to another, and also remembering to let go and let the **Harmonious Practice** (Right Effort or the 6R's) do its work.

8. Sammā Samādhi — Harmonious Collectedness- (Right Concentration):

Now we come to the part of the Eight-Fold Path that has many different interpretations and many different ideas attached to it.

The confusion starts by taking what some of the commentaries say and then placing too much emphasis on them.

Again, some commentaries are good and very useful and some don't agree so well with the foundation teachings of the Buddha.

The way to know for yourself whether a commentary is good to use or not is by comparing what is said with the suttas (discourses) and the vinaya (rules of discipline).

If they agree with the suttas and vinaya then one can be reasonably sure that these commentaries are reliable.

But when a commentary divides up the practice into many separate pieces it tends to make things very difficult to understand and practice, then it may be a good idea to let that kind of commentary stay on the bookshelf and be used as a reference book, instead of a main resource to follow.

NOTE: It is a good idea to use more than one sutta for comparing, in that way when many suttas seem to agree then you can be reasonably sure that this is the Buddha's Teachings.

Here is something very interesting about the words insight and serenity (Vipassanā/Samatha).

When we go to the Majjhima Nikāya, Middle Length Sayings (2nd edition, Wisdom Publications, Bhikkhu Bodhi's translation) and look up in the Index of Subjects the words "serenity and insight," we will see a striking similarity that shows that both of these words are used together almost ALWAYS!!!

On page 1397 the word "insight" is mentioned and has many suttas to go to for reference. Here are a few suttas so you can compare them: 6.3, 32.5, 43.14, 73.18, 77.29, 149.10, 151.19.

Then we go to the word "serenity" on page 1404 and these sutta references are 6.3, 32.5, 43.14, 73.18, 77.29, 149.10, 151.19.

Do you see the similarities in the numbers of the suttas and even the sections that they are being used in?

The point is that "serenity and insight" are almost always mentioned together and this gives us a clue that they are (as it says in sutta 149.10) yoked together.

This means that the Buddha was talking about one type of meditation practice that includes both serenity and insight (Samatha/Vipassanā) together at the same time!

Also, this means that the jhāna, which is so often mentioned in the suttas, is a very specific type of meditation level.

Why? This is because the kind of jhāna that the Buddha taught us is a Samatha/Vipassanā jhāna.

It is not to be confused with the ecstatic, or absorption type of one-pointed concentration jhāna, which is mostly being taught today.

The dividing up of Samatha and Vipassanā into two separate types of meditation tends to make the meditations quite complicated and one's progress, if it exists at all, seems to take a very long time.

This goes against one of the things that describes the brilliance of the Dhamma.

That is, the explanation that the Buddha's Teachings, are "immediately effective."

When that one extra step of relaxing and letting go of the craving is added, the meditator's progress in understanding and personality development and entire attitude toward all life seems to improve greatly, and reasonably quickly!

In the Dhammapada the Buddha said: "We are the Happy Ones!" and this is what happens when the meditator follows the instruction in meditation precisely, then relaxes, then smiles often.

The importance of practicing Samatha/Vipassanā meditation in exactly the same way as the suttas tell us to *can't be overstated!*

Why? Because if we don't add the extra step of relaxing one's mind and body on the in-breath and relaxing on the out-breath (which is the letting go of craving), then the meditation changes from being a Samatha/Vipassanā type of meditation to a one-pointed type of concentration.

They are different practices; they have different results.

When the one-pointed concentration is used, it suppresses the Hindrances (nīvaraṇa) by the force of the concentration. This includes access concentration (upacāra Samādhi) as well as absorption concentration (appaṇā samādhi).

The hindrances (nīvaraṇa) are where our attachments to a personal self are stored.

When one practices one-pointed concentration and the force of one's concentration pushes down a hindrance, it is not considered to be purifying the meditator's mind in the same way as the Buddha taught us to practice.

Anything that is suppressed is not let go of, but is stopped from arising while this strong concentration is present.

The suppressed hindrance has a real tendency to arise, even more strongly when the meditator's one-pointed concentration weakens.

With the practice of Samatha/Vipassanā or the letting go and then relaxing, over time the hindrance (nīvaraṇa) will fade away, never to arise again.

The Samatha/Vipassanā meditation is the way to actually purify one's mind.

During the time of the Buddha and after his death, the Brahmins were continually working to change the meditation, so that it agreed with their philosophies, concepts, and writings.

They took up using the word Jhāna and gave it their own definitions, which basically meant one-pointed concentration and they conveniently left out the one step that changes the entire meditation from Serenity/Insight (Samatha/Vipassanā) to a one-pointed concentration or absorption concentration.

Also, they took some of the most popular words and gave them different meanings just to confuse the issues.

According to Rhys-Davids, the word **"Samādhi"** was never used before the time of the Buddha.

The Buddha made this word up to describe Samatha/Vipassanā meditation which, when practiced in the way he describes it in the instructions, leads directly to Nibbāna!

Of course, during the time of the Buddha there were many words in Sanskrit to describe one-pointed concentration and this type of meditation went along very nicely with the Brahmin ways of practice.

When added to the meditation practice, this extra step of relaxing is the way to recognize and let go of Craving (Taṇhā).

This is why relaxing is so important and is specifically mentioned in so many suttas.

When we see that all of the Noble Truths are about letting go of Craving and relaxing of the tightness or tension in one's body and mind, it only makes sense to relax or tranquilize often, don't you agree?

Doesn't it seem to make sense to let go of craving as much as possible because it is the origin of suffering?

This is actively retraining and purifying Mind.

When the Buddha came along and chose the word "**Samādhi**" to describe Samatha/Vipassanā (Sammā Samādhi or Harmonious Collectedness), the Brahmins began to use this same word "Samādhi" with their own definition of one-pointed concentration.

This effectively divided the meditation of Samatha/Vipassanā and made it into two separate practices, that is, Samatha meditation and Vipassanā meditation.

The success in meditation and experiencing Nibbāna began to fade away about 1000 years after the Buddha's death, because commentaries chose to look at things in this way.

Because this was taken to be the way of meditation about 1,000 years after the Buddha's death (in some commentaries), the success in meditation and experiencing Nibbāna began to fade away.

Many different schools of thought began to argue philosophically about what was the correct way of practice, but, as you know, philosophy is the use of words without any action, and this began to change the whole way of looking at the Buddha's Teachings.

Let us now take a look at **Harmonious Collectedness** (Right Concentration). In the texts it mentions often that this fold of the Eight-Fold Path is the experiencing at least one if not all of the (Samatha/Vipassanā) jhāna.

I am going to add to each of these jhānas the type of jhāna one experiences.

The reason that I include the type of jhāna is so that there is no confusion about just what the Buddha taught as far as the jhāna is concerned.

The first (Samatha/Vipassanā) Jhāna as opposed to the first absorption jhāna;

the second (Samatha/Vipassanā) Jhāna as opposed to the second absorption jhāna;

the third (Samatha/Vipassanā) Jhāna as opposed to the third absorption jhāna; and

the fourth (Samatha/Vipassanā) Jhāna as opposed to the fourth absorption jhāna.

The four immaterial Jhānas (Arūpa Samatha/Vipassanā Jhānas) are included in the fourth jhāna, since they are different aspects of the deep equanimity found in the fourth jhāna.

Nowhere in the suttas does it say anything about the practice of Appana Samādhi—full absorption concentration, Upacāra Samādhi—Access or Neighborhood Concentration, or Khaṇikha Samadhi—Moment-to-moment concentration.

These are only mentioned in the Theravada commentaries and don't seem to agree with what the Suttas and Vinaya say about the way to attain the full understanding of how Dependent Origination or the Four Noble Truths actually occur.

You can see as we go along the Eight-Fold Path, these different folds are interwoven and are not separate parts to be taken apart and used.

The Entire Eight-Fold Path Works Together

The path works as an interconnected whole process of seeing, understanding, and letting go of all personal beliefs in a self.

In a way, you could see the different parts of the Eight-Fold Path as if they were separate pieces of a motor.

The motor won't run unless all of these parts are put together correctly.

When one uses all of the different folds of the Eight-Fold Path at the same time, this is the way of making this Path a good working tool.

Separately these "folds" may work to a limited degree, but when they are all folded together, they work extremely well.

Even today, Nibbāna can arise!

Unlocking the Door to the Deathless

The letting go of craving is the doorway to the deathless. Craving is the weak link in this process and the starting point towards reaching the Cessation of Suffering. The Path shows us exactly how to do this.

The simple explanation given in the Satipaṭṭhāna Sutta tells us to relax on the in-breath and to relax on the out-breath.

This simple act of <u>relaxing</u> both mind and body is following the entire Eight-Fold Path at exactly the same time.

This is the key for everyone to understand and unlock the door to the deathless.

Every time mind's attention moves slightly, **<u>craving is the cause</u>**.

Whenever the meditator releases and relaxes the tightness caused by this slight movement, purifying of the mind takes place and this leads directly to the final Cessation of all Suffering!

In other words, the Path that leads to the Cessation of Suffering is none other than this very Noble Eight-Fold Path, when it is used and practiced often!

As a result, mind becomes dispassionate and free from all craving and ignorance!

This is as true now in present times, as it was 2600 years ago.

Any instruction that does not emphasize the necessity for understanding Dependent Origination and the Four Noble Truths as its final goal of realization isn't teaching **the direct path**.

Currently, many people say that seeing impermanence, suffering, and not-self is realizing Nibbāna.

Please note, however, that although these characteristics are very important to develop--by themselves *they do not directly allow one to see the supramundane state of Nibbāna.*

This is a very important to ponder on!

A meditator can see one or all of the three characteristics of all existence, i.e., impermanence, suffering, and not-self, without ever directly seeing Dependent Origination, but one who sees Dependent Origination directly will always see all of the three characteristics.

According to the Mahā Vagga of the Vinaya, it cannot work any other way.

When meditators think deeply about this, they will see this for themselves!

In closing, this is the Buddha's advice to everyone:

**"There are these roots of trees, these empty huts.
Meditate!
Do not delay or else you will regret it later.
This is our instruction to you."**

(taken from the Majjhima Nikāya, Sutta 106.15)

The Courage to Investigate

Currently, there seem to be some disputes regarding the kinds of meditation the Buddha actually taught.

One school of thought says: "The meditator must begin by practicing Jhāna [fixed] concentration meditation and then proceed to the fourth jhāna [5] before switching over to the practice of vipassanā meditation or momentary concentration [khaṇikha Samadhi—straight vipassanā].

Other schools of thought say that one can attain Nibbāna without going through the jhāna[6], but only practice straight vipassanā meditation[7] or developing access concentration (upacāra samādhi) right from the beginning of their meditation practice.

Interestingly, the word "vipassanā" or "vidassana" (which has the same meaning) is mentioned only a very few times in the suttas and is almost always mentioned with samatha (Jhāna) practices.

For example: in sutta # 149:10 of the Majjhima Nikāya it says: **"These two things—*samatha and vipassanā* (serenity and insight)—occur in him yoked evenly together."**

The word "**jhāna**" (stage of understanding) is mentioned many thousands of times in the suttas.

So it is very apparent what the Buddha was teaching most, and it has to do with the practice of attaining jhāna while simultaneously using vipassanā (insight) in those states of understanding.

Moreover, the Ānāpānasati Sutta and Mindfulness of Mettā (loving-Kindness) shows that the Buddha taught only one kind of meditation, that is, by simultaneously developing both the jhāna and insight (samatha/vipassanā) through using the 6R's.

This sutta actually shows the method of how to tranquilize mind/body and develop wisdom at the same time by seeing the true nature of existence.

Through the eyes of the Four Noble Truths, while following this set pattern of investigation using the 6R's, a meditator observes the cause and effect relationship of Dependent Origination and by repeatedly witnessing anicca [impermanence], dukkha [suffering], and anattā [not-self], they come to understand "The true nature of everything."

At the same time, this practice of meditation fulfills the thirty-seven requisites of Awakening, which are: The Four Foundations of Mindfulness, the Four Kinds of Right Effort, the Four Bases of Spiritual Power, the Five Faculties, the Five Powers, the Seven Factors of Awakening, and the Noble Eight-Fold Path.

Please remember that using the 6R's is completing that part of the Eight-Fold Path called Right Effort or, as the author calls it, **Harmonious Practice.**

Hence, the way leading to the realization of the Supra-mundane Nibbāna is clearly and precisely taught in these wonderful suttas.

Some commentaries and sub-commentaries have divided "concentration" and "vipassanā" into two different forms of meditation.

This kind of "separation" does not appear in the suttas.

Although it is mentioned in one sutta in the Aṅguttara Nikāya that the first part of the practice is "samatha" and the second part is "vidassana" (developing wisdom or insight), this is not saying that there are two different types of practices or meditations.

The practice is exactly the same meditation with the same line of development aimed at the same end goal!

It is only that different things are seen at different times, as in the case of The Anupada Sutta, "One by One as they Occurred," from the Majjhima Nikāya, Sutta #111.

This sutta gives an explanation of Venerable Sāriputta meditation development and his experience in all the jhānas before he attained Arahantship.

In this wonderful sutta it explains that Venerable Sāriputta experienced the five aggregates, that is: body (body or contact), feeling (vedanā), perception (saññā), formations (saṅkhāra) and consciousness (viññāṇa), while he was in each of the jhāna states, i.e.,

He was experiencing vipassanā or insight into the true nature of phenomena while he was in each of the jhānas.

When one starts to divide, differentiate, and categorize meditation practices, the situation becomes very confusing.

This is also evident in the popular commentaries, such as the Vissudhi Magga and its sub-commentaries.

We begin to see inconsistencies when we make a comparison with the suttas and these commentaries.

Nowadays, most scholars use just a line or parts of a sutta to ensure that the commentaries agree with the suttas.

However, if one were to read the sutta as a whole, often times the sutta has an entirely different meaning.

This is not to say that scholars are intentionally making wrong statements.

However, sometimes they are caught in looking at such tiny details or parts of the Dhamma with such an unwavering view that they tend to lose sight of the larger picture of the overall teaching.

By doing that, the end results are always different from the core meaning of the suttas.

The description of the jhānas or levels of understanding in the Vissudhi Magga don't exactly match the description given in the suttas.

For example, the Vissudhi Magga talks about having a sign (nimittas in Pāli) of some kind of visualized, mind-made object which arises in mind at certain times during the practice of absorption meditation.

However, the Bodhisatta (future Buddha) firmly rejected this form of strongly focused concentration as leading the way to Nibbāna!

If one were to check the suttas, the idea of strongly focusing on nimittas arising in mind has never been mentioned.

If it were very important, it would be mentioned many times.

The Buddha never taught absorption concentration techniques having nimittas (signs) arising to be constantly observed, *nor did he teach the chanting of mantras or repeating of words mentally.*

These are forms of Hindu Brahmin practices that have crept into Buddhism for hundreds of years.

Their influences can be seen in one-pointed concentration practices.

Most especially we find them in the Tibetan Buddhist styles of meditation as well as in other popular commentaries like the Vissudhi Magga.

Thus, many approaches to the meditation, especially one-pointed concentration, do not conform to the instructions or results given in the suttas.

To be successful, the meditator must honestly and openly investigate for themselves what is being said and then check it against the suttas.

It is best that the meditator does not use only part of a sutta to do this, but investigates the whole sutta to avoid confusion.

It is also very important to check for oneself if what is mentioned in one sutta matches what other suttas say about the same subject.

For example: In the sutta # 20 of the Middle Length Discourses (Majjhima Nikāya) published by Wisdom Publications the sutta called "The Removal of Distracting Thoughts" says in section # 7:

If while he is giving attention to stilling the thought-formations of those thoughts, there still arises in him evil unwholesome thoughts connected with desire, with hate, with delusion,

then, with his teeth clenched and his tongue pressed against the roof of his mouth, he should beat down, constrain, and crush mind with mind....

Now we go to another sutta # 36:20 that is talking about the Bodhisatta's search for awakening and it says:

"I thought, suppose with my teeth clenched and my tongue pressed against the roof of my mouth, I beat down, constrain, and crush mind with mind....

While I did that sweat ran from my armpits.

Just as a strong man might seize a weaker man by the head or shoulders and beat him down, constrain him, and crush him, so too, with my teeth clenched and my tongue pressed to the roof of my mouth, I beat down, constrained, and crushed mind with mind, and sweat ran from my armpits.

But although tireless energy was aroused in me and unremitting mindfulness was established, my body was overwrought and uncalm because I was exhausted, by the painful striving.

Sutta #36 definitely shows that this is not the way to overcome a hindrance.

But it is a recommended practice given in sutta #20 and is given by many meditation teachers for their students to use! How can that be?

The answer is when one practices an absorption or one-pointed type of concentration the meditator is not able to see or recognize a hindrance when or how it arises.

When it does arise, they think a hindrance is supposed to be fought with and forcibly suppressed!

As the reader has hopefully seen in earlier chapters of this book, a hindrance is not to be fought with or brutally suppressed.

The hindrance is your teacher.

When it arises it should be seen as an opportunity to observe HOW it arises, so that the meditator can see its true nature, i.e. the impersonal (anattā) process of Dependent Origination and the Four Noble Truths.

Does the reader see the differences in these two approaches to the meditation practice?

Perhaps sutta # 20 was copied from sutta #36, because the person who did this was practicing absorption or one-pointed concentration and had problems with some hindrances, so they added this to that sutta as a solution.

But, this is the only place in all of the suttas that this technique is mentioned as the solution to troublesome hindrances.

There are no other suttas to support this idea.

Therefore, it is not out of place to consider this to be a later addition to this sutta and should be suspect and not to be blindly followed.

Of course, this is the author's opinion and if a meditator wants to try crushing mind with mind, please feel free to do so.

Also if you find that it works for you, please let the author know about it, so you can show the advantages of such a painful technique.

Sutta #36 shows all kinds of meditations that the Bodhisatta practiced that did not work before he finally came upon a practice that did work.

The working practice that brought success to the Bodhisatta are the ones mentioned in this book.

It must also be said that, if a person is sincerely looking for the truth, sometimes even one line from a sutta may bring deep understanding.

The bottom line is that there is always a need for careful examination!

When a meditator honestly questions what the Buddha's Teachings really are, they will observe that open investigation helps them to see more clearly.

Thus, questions can be answered rationally and inconsistencies will disappear in most cases.

Always remember that the commentaries and sub-commentaries are an author's interpretation of what the suttas say and mean.

Even this book is full of commentary by the author and hopefully it is helpful and correct.

Many times monks with the best intentions have searched for new ways to expand their understanding and attempt to help others to make progress.

Then, as time goes by, scholars may choose to expound on a certain comment, here or there, expanding the meaning in subtle ways that leave the original text behind.

For example: In sutta #43:9 of the Majjhima Nikāya 'The Greater Series of Questions and Answers' in section #9 it says:

> *Feeling, perception, and consciousness...are conjoined, not disjoined, and it is impossible to separate each of these states from the others in order to describe the difference between them. For what one feels, that one perceives, and what one perceives, that one cognizes.*

Now, according to the above quotation from the sutta, feeling, perception, and consciousness cannot be separated.

The author has seen many articles and books talking about feeling only or about perception only!

But the sutta above states that one cannot talk about one of these things without including the others.

Can anyone state that the monks who have written these articles are mistaken? Not really!

Because their intention is to explore more thoroughly how things occur and they want to give definitions to every little part of the Dhamma.

There is no blame for their intention here, for sure!

When any person over-divides things, they tend to miss the point of the main idea that the Buddha was teaching us.

Therein lies the problem.

This over-dividing of the teachings "dilutes" the true teaching and thus has the tendency to take the meditator further away from the true meaning and understanding of the suttas.

As a result, many puzzling questions arise.

For example: "In the practice of momentary concentration (straight vipassanā - khaṇikha samādhi), where does Dependent Origination fit into the scheme of things?"

This practice doesn't seem to go hand in hand with the teaching of Dependent Origination.

Another question is: "According to the suttas, Right Effort means bringing up wholesome, joyful interest, or enthusiasm (chanda) in mind.

Contrary to this, some say Right Effort only means "noting."

Other puzzling questions that one might ask are, "Which suttas mentioned the terms momentary [Khaṇikha

Samadhi], access [Upacāra Samādhi], and absorption or fixed concentration [Appana Samādhi]?"

"Which sutta describes Insight Knowledges only"?

"Which sutta says that there is no mindfulness while in the jhāna meditation stage?"

Please note that in the Parinibbāna Sutta, the Lord Buddha requested his disciples to always check against the suttas and Vinaya, not any other texts.

There comes a time when the meditators and teachers must stop repeating the words of others.

It might be wise to transpose the practice of questionable methods of meditation by themselves and take time out to do some open and honest investigation of the original teachings of the Buddha.

Doesn't this sound reasonable?

One must not depend on hearsay or blind belief in what a teacher says simply because they are the authority.

In the Kalama Sutta, the Buddha gives some very good advice:

> *It is unwise to simply believe what one hears because it has been said over and over again for a long time.*
>
> *It is unwise to follow tradition blindly just because it has been practiced in that way for a long time.*
>
> *It is unwise to listen to and spread rumors and gossip.*

It is unwise to take anything as being the absolute truth just because it agrees with one's scriptures (this especially means commentaries and sub-commentaries in Buddhism).

It is unwise to foolishly make assumptions, without investigation.

It is unwise to abruptly draw a conclusion by what one sees and hears without further investigation.

It is unwise to go by mere outward appearances or to hold too tightly to any view or idea simply because one is comfortable with it.

It is unwise to be convinced of anything out of respect and deference to one spiritual teacher (without honest investigation into what is being taught).

It is unwise for anyone to say, "This is the belief of this faith to believe in and only this is true, anything else is wrong".

If we are to be true investigators of this path, we must go beyond opinions, beliefs, and dogmatic thinking.

In this way, we can rightly reject anything which when accepted, practiced, and perfected, leads to more anger, criticism, conceit, pride, greed, and/or delusion.

These unwholesome states of mind are universally condemned and are certainly not beneficial to us or to others.

They are to be avoided whenever possible.

On the other hand, we can rightly accept anything which when practiced and perfected, leads to unconditional love, collectedness, contentment, and gentle wisdom.

These things allow us to develop a happy, collected, tranquil, and peaceful mind.

Thus, the wise praise all kinds of unconditional love (loving acceptance of the present moment), tranquility, collectedness, contentment and gentle wisdom and encourages everyone to practice these good qualities as much as possible.

Please don't believe anything you read here, but try the meditation and see if it works well or not.

In the Canki sutta #95:14 in the Middle Length Discourses (Majjhima Nikāya) this is cleared up even further. As updated by the author, it says:

> *There are five things...that may turn out in two different ways here and now. What five?*
>
> *Faith, approval, oral tradition, reasoned consideration, and reflective acceptance of a view. These five things may turn out in two different ways here and now.*
>
> *Now something may be fully accepted out of faith, yet it may be empty, hollow, and false; but something else may not be fully accepted out of faith, yet it may be factual, true, and unmistaken.*
>
> *Again, something may be fully approved of, yet it may be empty, hollow, and false; but*

*something else may not be fully approved of,
yet it may be factual, true, and unmistaken.*

*Again, something may be well transmitted, yet
it may be empty, hollow, and false; but
something else may not be well transmitted
yet it may be factual, true, and unmistaken.*

*Again, something may be well considered, yet
it may be empty, hollow, and false; but
something else may not be well considered yet
it may be factual, true, and unmistaken.*

*Again, something may be well reflected upon,
yet it may be empty, hollow, and false; but
something else may not be well reflected
upon, yet it may be factual, true, and
unmistaken.*

*Under these conditions it is not proper for a
wise man who preserves truth to come to the
definite conclusion: 'Only this is true,
anything else is wrong.'*

*One preserves truth when they say: 'My faith
is such and such' but he does not come to the
definite conclusion, 'Only this is true and
anything else is wrong'.*

Only by the meditator's direct experience and study of the
suttas will they come to know what is right and correct.

This is true if the meditator follows the meditation
instructions without subtracting or adding anything or
changing things to suit themselves.

The author has found the Buddha's precise meditation instructions to match up with the suttas guidelines.

Many commentarial writings seem to lead meditators astray from the original intent of the Buddha's meditation practice.

By saying this, the author still does not say, "Only this is true and everything else is wrong."

Please search for yourself and see if this is true for you also!

In the Parinibbāna Sutta, the Buddha's advice to the monks is very plain and precise.

The meditator is to practice according to the scriptural texts and observe whether the practice is done correctly.

Only after direct experience and close examination can the meditator be sure that the scriptures are correct.

Thus, the Buddha's advice to the monks is not only to use the suttas, but also to check whether the suttas are correct according to the Dhamma (sutta) and the Discipline (Vinaya).

This is how a meditator makes sure that the information is true and can then be practiced correctly.

This is taken from Sutta number 16, section 4.7 to 4.11 of the Digha Nikāya translated from the book "Thus Have I Heard" by Maurice Walsh. It says:

> *4.7] At Bhogangagara the Lord stayed at the Ananda Shrine. And here he said to the monks: "Monks, I will teach you four criteria. Listen, pay close attention, and I will speak.'*
> *'Yes, Lord,' replied the monks.*

4.8] "Suppose a monk were to say: 'Friends, I heard and received this from the Buddha's own lips:

This is the Dhamma, this is the Discipline, this is the Master's teaching', then monks, you should neither approve nor disapprove his words.

Then, without approving or disapproving, his words and expressions should be carefully noted and compared with the Suttas and reviewed in the light of the Discipline.

If they, on such comparison and review, are found not to conform to the Suttas and the Discipline, the conclusion must be:

"Assuredly this is not the word of the Buddha, it has been wrongly understood by this monk"; and the matter is to be rejected.

But in here on such comparison and review they are found to conform to the Suttas and the Discipline, the conclusion must be:

"Assuredly this is the word of the Buddha, it has been rightly understood by this monk."

This is the first criterion.

4.9] "Suppose a monk were to say:

"In such and such a place there is a community with elders and distinguished teachers, who know the Dhamma, the Discipline - the code of rules:

I have heard and received this from that
community';

then, monks you should neither approve nor
disapprove his words.

Then, without approving or disapproving, his
words and expressions should be carefully
noted and compared with the Suttas and
reviewed in the light of the Discipline.

If they, on such comparison and review, are
found not to conform to the Suttas and
Discipline, the conclusion must be:

"Assuredly this is not the word of the
Buddha, it has been wrongly understood by
this monk'; and the matter is to be rejected.

But where on such comparison and review they
are found to conform to the Dhamma and the
Discipline, the conclusion must be:

"Assuredly this is the word of the Buddha, it
has been rightly understood by this monk."

That is the second criterion.

4.10] "Suppose a monk were to say:

"In such and such a place there are many
elders who are learned, bearers of the
tradition, who know the Dhamma, the
Discipline - the code of rules:

I have heard and received this from those monks, you should neither approve nor disapprove his words.

Then, without approving or disapproving, his words and expressions should be carefully noted and compared with the Suttas and reviewed in the light of the Discipline.

If they, on such comparison and review, are found not to conform to the Suttas and Discipline, the conclusion must be:

"Assuredly this is not the word of the Buddha, it has been wrongly understood by this monk'; and the matter is to be rejected.

But where on such comparison and review they are found to conform to the Suttas and Discipline, the conclusion must be:

"Assuredly this is the word of the Buddha, it has been rightly understood by this monk"; and the matter is to be accepted.

This is the third criterion.

4.11] "Suppose a monk were to say: "In such and such a place there is one elder who is learned. Who knows the Dhamma, and the Discipline - the code of rules.

I have heard and received this from that elder, you should neither approve nor disapprove his words.

Then, without approving or disapproving, his words and expressions should be carefully noted and compared with the Suttas and reviewed in the light of the Discipline.

If they, on such comparison and review, are found not to conform to the Suttas and Discipline, the conclusion must be:

"Assuredly this is not the word of the Buddha, it has been wrongly understood by this monk'; and the matter is to be rejected.

But where on such comparison and review they are found to conform to the Suttas and Discipline, the conclusion must be:

"Assuredly this is the word of the Buddha, it has been rightly understood by this monk'; and the matter is to be accepted.

This is the fourth criterion.

The Spirit of Open Investigation

The spirit of open investigation and exploration into the ways and means of the Buddha's Middle Path is open to all who have an inquiring mind.

This means a mind which is not stuck in looking at things through pride and attachment at what they "think" is right without first checking with the suttas.[8]

Occasionally, some meditators and teachers become over-attached to their opinions such that they think their method is the "only way," without checking the true teachings from the suttas.

This can be going on even when meditators are not successfully reaching their goals and have not heard of anyone proven to be truly successful.

Those who have the courage to investigate and practice what is suggested in this book will be pleasantly surprised at the simplicity and clarity of the Buddha's teaching.

Although the suttas appear dry and repetitive, they are quite illuminating and can be fun to read, especially when the meditator practices the meditation and gains experiential and intellectual knowledge at the same time.

As a matter of fact, the author is spending time putting the repetitions back into the suttas and simplifying some of the words.

This is being done because if recited to sincere meditators the suttas become clear and set in one's mind and this energizes their practice.

After hearing a Dhamma talk given in this way, as the meditator begins to sit, it will help them to observe the way the Buddha taught, and their progress is much faster.

The thing to remember here is that the Buddha's teachings were originally an oral tradition and repetition was a necessary part.

As the author has seen firsthand, this is still as true today as it was 2600 years ago

Prelude to Tranquil Wisdom
Insight (TWIM or Samatha/Vipassanā) Meditation

Before the meditator starts meditating, it is very important to build a strong foundation of morality (sīla).

The author knows very well how much people in the West don't like to hear this!

OK. So here's the thing about this topic.

The precepts contain **"the needed operational advice,"** so that the meditation can run smoothly.

It is clearly apparent that this practice moves steadily towards attaining Knowledge and Wisdom of the True Nature of Everything.

Having said this, if the meditator is going to take the time and effort to do this practice, then it only makes sense to follow all of the instructions given by the Buddha, don't you think?

For the meditator who breaks the precepts, it is almost useless for them to take up the practice of meditation. Why?

Because if someone breaks the precepts during their daily life, they will have to spend a lot of time and energy before their mind is pure enough to have any progress in meditation.

Breaking precepts leads to more hindrances arising and slow progress.

It is that simple!

Meditators who want to have progress in their meditation have to be willing to change old, unwholesome habits into new, wholesome habits and following the precepts is the way to accomplish this.

Meditation is not about just sitting quietly and having peace and joy arising.

It is not about escaping the world.

It is about learning how to have an uplifted, balanced mind all of the time so that the meditator is ready to accept the liberation of being free from ignorance and craving, and living happily!

Your choice to make!

The willingness to change and become more content with life results in the candy that makes life so much fun!

The meditators who don't practice the five precepts will lose interest and finally stop meditating because they think that this technique is incorrect.

Actually the Buddha's technique works very well.

If it isn't working, then, the meditator is neither doing the complete practice nor is it being done in the correct way.

Keeping the precepts during daily activities without breaking them prepares the way for a natural development resulting in "purity of mind."

If the meditator breaks any of these precepts, as a backlash, they will experience restlessness, remorse, anger, fear, and anxiety due to arising guilty feelings.

Their meditation will become difficult and progress is almost non-existent.

Therefore, following the precepts is like preparing an engine to run smoothly; to have successful meditation.

Again, this is your choice.

No one else can make it for you.

Here is another important aspect of meditation that needs to be looked at and followed!

Please *practice only one meditation technique at a time,* because mind will become confused if the meditator tries to mix and match various meditation techniques.

The author does understand the attraction to using two or three techniques.

For instance, the meditator may want to get some exercise by doing Yoga or Tai Chi, investigating kundalini practices, as well as remote viewing, and even psycho-therapy techniques, but if real progress is desired, it is best to do just one practice at a time until it is extremely stable.

These other practices have forms of one-pointed concentration in them that can eventually cause problems when the meditator gets into the subtler states of aware samatha/vipassanā jhāna.

There is no question that exercise is good for a person mentally and physically. The author has no objection to doing a physical exercise, such as Yoga or Tai Chi, as a short morning form expressly for the purpose of health, as long as the meditator includes the Release, Relax, Smile steps of the 6R's into that practice and is carefully not over focusing on one particular thing.

The most important thing to understand here is that mind is habitually trained in a pattern of behavior and the meditator is now attempting to "purify" mind by re-training it into a new pattern of behavior.

Getting involved with multiple practices to train mind only confuses it more.

The most effective direct route to purification of mind is taking the single most direct route to the desired destination.

That route is discussed here in this book.

This is not a judgment or a condemnation of these other practices in any way at all.

This is simply an observation of how successful meditation comes to be, and after many years, the author has uncovered this practice and teaching which leads to reaching the end of suffering.

Mixing and matching practices only slows down or even stops the meditator's progress and can cause confusion for mind.

The mixing of one-pointed concentration while doing the Tranquil Wisdom Insight Meditation (TWIM) slows down meditation progress so much that it seems there is no progress at all.

In the Digha Nikāya sutta #28 of section #10 it talks about the modes of progress in the Buddha's teachings. It says:

> **Also unsurpassed is the Blessed one's way of teaching Dhamma in regard to the modes of progress, which are four:**
>
> *painful progress with slow comprehension; painful progress with quick comprehension; pleasant progress with slow comprehension; pleasant progress with quick comprehension.*
>
> *In the case of painful progress with slow comprehension, it is considered poor on account of both painfulness and slow comprehension.*
>
> *In the case of painful progress with quick comprehension, it is considered <u>poor</u> on account of painfulness.*
>
> *In the case of pleasant progress with slow comprehension, it is considered <u>poor</u> on account of slow comprehension.*

In the case of pleasant progress and quick comprehension, it is considered <u>excellent</u> on account of both pleasantness and quick comprehension.

This is the unsurpassed teaching in regard to the modes of progress.

This is how the meditator judges whether or not they are following the path leading to the Cessation of Suffering in the correct way.

Meditation is supposed to be fun and when it is done correctly the meditator actually looks forward to doing their sitting meditation because they learn so much.

Finding a Guiding Teacher for Your Meditation Training

How does the meditator find a good meditation guide?

Did the Buddha leave us any information about finding a teacher and practicing meditation with them?

It appears that the best way is to pick only the meditation teacher who truly understands the meditation and Dependent Origination and can teach it.

In the Saṃyutta Nikāya II.12.82, The Book of Causation, Page 620, it says:

"Monks, the meditator who does not know and see as it actually is aging-and-death (jarā-maraṇa) its origin, its cessation, and the way leading to its cessation, should search for a teacher in order to know this as it actually is."

Please notice that the Four Noble Truths are mentioned in each of the links here.

The truths are used here as deductive investigation.

The First Noble Truth is equal to examining suffering.

Investigating the link's origin/cause is equivalent to the Second Noble Truth;

Investigating that link's cessation is the equivalent to the Third Noble Truth;

The way leading to the cessation of that link, is the Fourth Noble Truth.

This is how a meditator realizes the Four Noble Truths and investigates all phenomena as they arise and cease (expanded text).

> *"Monks, one who does not know and see as it actually is birth, (Jāti) its origin, its cessation, and the way leading to its cessation, should search for a teacher in order to know this as it actually is."*

> *"Monks, one who does not know and see as it actually is habitual tendency, (bhava) its origin, its cessation, and the way leading to its cessation, should search for a teacher in order to know this as it actually is."*

> *"Monks, one who does not know and see as it actually is clinging, (upādāna) its origin, its cessation, and the way leading to its cessation, should search for a teacher in order to know this as it actually is."*

> *"Monks, one who does not know and see as it actually is craving, (taṇhā) its origin, its cessation, and the way leading to its*

cessation, should search for a teacher in order to know this as it actually is."

"Monks, one who does not know and see as it actually is feeling, (vedanā) its origin, its cessation, and the way leading to its cessation, should search for a teacher in order to know this as it actually is."

"Monks, one who does not know and see as it actually is contact, (phassa) its origin, its cessation, and the way leading to its cessation, should search for a teacher in order to know this as it actually is."

"Monks, one who does not know and see as it actually is the six sense bases, (saḷāyatana) their origin, their cessation, and the way leading to their cessation, should search for a teacher in order to know this as it actually is."

"Monks, one who does not know and see as it actually is mentality/materiality, (nāma-rūpa) their origin, their cessation, and the way leading to their cessation, should search for a teacher in order to know this as it actually is."

"Monks, one who does not know and see as it actually is consciousness, (viññāṇa) its origin, its cessation, and the way leading to its cessation, should search for a teacher in order to know this as it actually is."

"Monks, one who does not know and see as it actually is formations, (saṅkhāra) their origin, their cessation, and the way leading to their cessation, should search for a teacher in order to know this as it actually is."

"Monks, one who does not know and see as it actually is ignorance, (avijjā) its origin, its cessation, and the way leading to its cessation, should search for a teacher in order to know as it actually is."

 This is the advice that the Buddha has given concerning finding a guiding teacher.

The most helpful guiding teacher will turn out to be someone who understands precisely how Dependent Origination occurs and how this understanding can be applied in daily life.

Also, another way to select a good teacher is by observing if their students are kind, pleasant, friendly, and supportive.

Then, the meditator should stay with that teacher for a period of time to verify what he finds.

The meditator should only practice what is being taught, and see whether mind becomes more clear, happy, and peaceful all of the time; not just while meditating, but in daily life as well.

This is ultimately the best way to choose a guiding teacher.

After a time, ask yourself:

Is your awareness of mind states becoming clearer and easier to recognize and are you able to let go of them by practicing Right Effort (6R's) during your daily activities as well as during your sitting sessions?

Are you able to smile more easily in daily life and to let things go?

If this isn't happening, then check in with the teacher and the suttas to see if what is being taught agrees with them or not.

As the meditator's practice deepens and the meditation becomes better, the suttas become clearer and easier to understand.

This always happens when the teacher is using the suttas as their guide.

The Five Hindrances

Lastly, it is very important for the meditator to recognize HOW the five hindrances arise.

They are:

1. lust or greed (lobha),
2. hatred or aversion (dosa),
3. sloth and torpor or sleepiness and dullness (thina – middha),
4. restlessness, scatteredness, remorse or anxiety (uddhacca – kukucca)
5. and perplexity or doubt (vicikiccha).

A hindrance is an obstacle or a distraction, because it completely stops the meditator from practicing meditation while sitting or in their daily activities.

A hindrance also causes the meditator to take whatever arises personally (attā) instead of impersonally (anattā).

In the early stages of training, whenever these hindrances arise, the meditator doesn't realize that they tend to identify with them very strongly and take them personally, i.e., "I am sleepy, I am restless, I like and I want, I dislike and I hate, I have doubt."

These hindrances completely cloud the meditator's mind and stop mind from seeing clearly whatever happens in the present moment due to the ego involvement of "I am that" (craving).

When the meditator is practicing "fixed or absorption concentration" the meditator lets go of any distraction and then immediately redirects their attention back to the meditation object again.

In this way, the absorption meditator *brings back the craving to their meditation object* and therein lies the real difference between these two forms of meditation.

On the other hand, when practicing Tranquil Wisdom Insight Meditation (TWIM), the meditator lets go of the distraction, but then they add a step to relax any leftover tension or tightness in the head.

Because of this extra step they feel mind become open, expanded, clear, and calm, without any distracting thoughts.

It is at this point the meditator is actually letting go of craving! (the Third Noble Truth).

Only then does the meditator smile and redirect their attention back to the object of meditation (i.e., the mettā meditation and relaxing OR the breath and relaxing on both the in and out-breath).

Over the past fifteen years, the author has developed a training pattern to assist the student in practicing this technique, which is in line with the suttas and which improves the meditator's mindfulness very much.

This method was actually given to him by one of his students while on retreat.

It started out as 5R's, then the author added one more R to complete the whole process.

This is called "the 6R's"—which is a different way of showing how Right Effort works!

That is, to **recognize** when an unwholesome state arises; **release** (let go of) that state and **relax**; bring up a wholesome state **re-smile;** and **return** mind's attention back to the object of meditation; then **repeat** staying on the object of meditation for as long as possible.

The relax step changes the whole meditation from a fixed or absorbed concentration technique to a more flowing, mindful, and calm kind of awareness, that doesn't go as deep as the absorption concentration types of meditation, nor does it suppress the hindrances although, eventually, they do fall away.

The result is that the meditator becomes more in tune with the teachings in the suttas as mind continually opens up on each relax step.

In Buddhist meditation, have any of these questions ever come up for you?

> "What is mindfulness (Sati), really?"
> "Exactly how does a person practice being mindful?"
> "Can mindfulness really lighten up the meditator's perspective and help bring joy, happiness, and balance into every aspect of life?"

If mindfulness is "remembering how to observe, step-by-step, how mind's attention moves away from whatever you are doing whenever a distraction arises," then the meditator is practicing mindfulness correctly.

If you continue doing this within daily activities or during sitting meditation practice, life becomes easier and more stress free.

Because of the relief we uncover, it seems that this would be a useful tool to develop. Don't you agree?

To clearly understand this connection and to achieve successful meditation, the meditator has to start with a precise definition of Meditation (bhavana) and Mindfulness (Sati).

Seeing this will help the meditator gain a new **Harmonious Perspective** (Sammā Diṭṭhi).

It will show us how mind works and "HOW" the meditator can change old painful habits that cause great suffering into a new way of having a contented, balanced mind.

This is the point of all of the Buddha's teachings, isn't it?

While practicing this meditation in all of life, the meditator begins to see clearly why it seems like arising hindrances are the enemy to fight with.

The Two Oxen with Picture of Oxen and Gate!

To understand how the hindrances are our teachers, showing us where our true attachments actually are, the meditator has to understand fully how Meditation and Mindfulness are interconnected for proper operation.

Let's look at the definition of Meditation first.

> **Meditation (bhavana) is "observing how mind's attention moves moment-to-moment, in order to see clearly and precisely "HOW" the impersonal (anattā) process of Dependent Origination (paṭiccasamuppāda) and the Four Noble Truths occur."**

Seeing and understanding "HOW" mind's attention moves from one thing to another is what the main thrust is in Buddhist Meditation!

This is why Dependent Origination is so important to see and understand within a usable context.

This practice naturally leads the meditator to develop a true impersonal (anattā) perspective.

They come to see that precise observation of the impersonal arising phenomena leads them to see for themselves the true nature of ALL existence.

Why is this important?

Because concerning awakening, it has been said by the Blessed One:

> **One who sees Dependent Origination sees the Dhamma; One who sees the Dhamma sees Dependent Origination. [MN-28:28]**

Could it be that this is what the Buddha meant when he referred to Wisdom?

Could it have meant understanding this most important truth?

Now, let's look at mindfulness.

> **Mindfulness means "remembering" to observe mind's attention as it moves moment-to-moment and remembering what to do with any arising phenomena!"**

This is why successful meditation needs a highly developed skill of mindfulness!

These two parts, meditation and mindfulness, are concomitant.

They cannot come to fulfillment without being yoked together.

Learning the 6R's Process

The "6R's" training is a reclaimed ancient guidance system the Buddha called Right Effort, which develops this skill.

The first "R" is to **RECOGNIZE** when mind has become distracted.

Before we do this step, the meditator must remember to use their observation power for the meditation cycle to start running.

Mindfulness is the fuel. It's just like gas for an engine. Without Mindfulness, everything stops!

To begin this cycle "smoothly" the meditator must have lots of gas in the tank to start the engine!

As the meditator continues meditation (bhavana) they realize that this helps a person to let go of delusion.

According to the Buddha, delusion means "taking things that arise personally and identifying with them to be I/Me/Mine. In Pāli this is "attā."

When the meditator understands this, then they will begin to let go of difficult delusional states in life, such as "my" fear, "my" worry, "my" anger, "my" tension, "my" stress, "my" anxiety, "my" depression, "my" sadness, "my" sorrow, "my" fatigue, "my" condemnation, "my" feelings of helplessness, or whatever "my" catch of the day happens to be (attachment).

This "unharmonious personal perspective" (wrong view) is a large part of what causes suffering.

This view arises from misunderstanding how things occur.

The "6R's" are steps which, when practiced, evolve into one fluid motion, creating a new wholesome habitual tendency that relieves any dis-ease in mind and body.

The cycle begins when MINDFULNESS recollects the 6R's which are:

RECOGNIZE
RELEASE
RELAX
RE-SMILE
RETURN
REPEAT

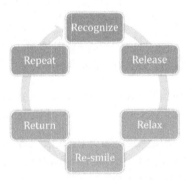

Once the meditator understands what the purpose of mindfulness is, keeping it going all the time is no longer problematic and this makes the meditation easier to understand, plus it is much more "fun" to practice.

It becomes a part of happy living and this brings up a smile.

By remembering to use the 6R's, this leads to having a wholesome up-lifted mind.

Therefore, this recollection process (mindfulness) is very important.

Remember to gas-up the engine so it can run smoothly.

That's the trick!

Now we begin to:

RECOGNIZE: This step is where the meditator becomes aware of the movement of mind's attention.

The meditator will begin to notice a slight sensation of tension or tightness as mind's attention barely begins to move toward any arising phenomena.

Pleasant or painful feeling can occur at any one of the six sense doors.

Any sight, sound, odor, taste, touch, or thought can cause this pulling sensation to begin.

With careful non-judgmental observation, the meditator will notice a slight tightening sensation.

Early *recognition* of this movement is vital to successful meditation.

The meditator then continues on to:

RELEASE: When a feeling or thought arises, the meditator *releases* it; let's it be there without giving any more attention to it.

The content of the distraction is not important at all, but the mechanics of HOW it arises are important!

Just let go of any tightness around it; let it be there without keeping attention on it.

Mind's attention is the nutriment or food for craving and clinging to arise.

Without attention, the clinging passes away from a lack of food.

Mindfulness then reminds the meditator to;

RELAX: After releasing the feeling or sensation, and allowing it to be, without trying to control it; there is a subtle, barely noticeable tension within mind/body.

This is why a RELAX [tranquilization] step is being pointed out by the Buddha in his meditation instructions.

PLEASE, DON'T SKIP THIS STEP!

It would be like forgetting to put oil in a car, so that the motor can run smoothly.

The important Pāli word here is "**pas'sambaya**."

As it is used in the suttas, this word specifically means "to tranquilize" and appears as an action verb to be performed.

This is not a general kind of relaxed or tranquilized feeling that can arise with other kinds of meditations.

This point is sometimes misunderstood in translation, which then changes the end result!

Without performing this step of relaxation every time in the cycle of meditation, the meditator will not experience a close-up view of the ceasing (cessation) of the tension caused by craving or feel that relief as the tightness is relaxed.

Note that *craving always first manifests as a tightness or tension in both the meditator's mind (nāma) and body (rūpa).*

The meditator has a momentary opportunity to see and experience the true nature and relief of cessation (of tightness and suffering) while performing the RELEASE/RELAX steps.

Mindfulness moves on with a recollection the meditator should then:

RE-SMILE: If you have listened to the Dhamma talks at www.dhammasukha.org, you might remember hearing about how smiling is an important aspect for the meditation.

Learning to smile with mind and raising slightly the corners of the mouth helps mind to be observant, alert, and agile.

Getting serious, tensing up, or frowning causes mind to become heavy and the meditator's mindfulness becomes dull and slow.

Insights become more difficult to see when the meditator is serious, thus slowing down understanding of the Dhamma.

Imagine, for a moment, the young Bodhisatta resting under the Rose Apple Tree as a young boy.

He was not serious and tense when he attained a pleasant abiding (samatha/vipassanā jhāna) and had deep insights with a light mind.

Want to see clearly? It's easy! Just lighten up, have fun exploring and smile! Smiling leads us to a happier more interesting practice.

If the meditator forgets to Release/Relax, rather than punishing or criticizing themselves, they should be kind, re-smile, and start again.

Keeping up our humor, pure sense of fun, exploration, and recycling is important.

After re-smiling, mindfulness recalls the next step.

RETURN or RE-DIRECT: Gently re-direct mind's attention back to the object of meditation (that is the breath and relaxing, or mettā and relaxing) continuing with a gentle collected mind to use that object as a "**home base.**"

In daily life, having been pulled off task, this is where the meditator returns their attention back to releasing, relaxing, and re-smiling into the task.

Sometimes people say this practice cycle is simpler than expected!

In history, simple things can become a mystery through small changes and omissions!

Reclaiming this practice develops more effective focus (mindfulness) on daily tasks with less tension and tightness.

The meditator's mindfulness improves through practice in daily activities.

Mind becomes more naturally balanced and happy.

The meditator becomes more efficient at whatever they do in life and, actually, they have more fun doing all of the things that used to be drudgery.

Nearing the end of the cycle, Mindfulness helps with a final recollection to:

REPEAT: Repeat this entire practice of staying with the object of meditation to attain the results the Buddha said could be reached in this lifetime!

Repeating the "6R's cycle" over and over again eventually replaces old habitual suffering, as we see and experience for ourselves what suffering actually is;

Notice the cause, which is becoming involved with the tension and tightness in any way;

experience how to reach the cessation by releasing and relaxing;

and discover how to exercise the direct path to that Cessation of Suffering.

This happens each time the meditator Releases an arising feeling, Relaxes, and Re-smiles. Notice the Relief.

Sharpening the skill of mindfulness is *the key* to simple and smooth meditation.

In summary, Mindfulness is *very* relevant to Buddhist meditation and daily life.

The process of recollection keeps the 6 steps of the practice moving.

Practicing this meditation as close to the description found in the suttas as possible will lighten all of life's experiences.

A very similar practice was taught to people in the time of the Buddha.

The remarkable results of doing the meditation in this way are "immediately effective" for anyone who diligently and ardently embraces these instructions.

When the meditator has an attachment arise (personal perspective or attā), this practice will eventually dissolve such hindrances.

It does take persistent and constant use of the "6R's" to have this happen.

When practicing in this way, it changes the meditator's perspective and leads to a more successful, happy, and peaceful experience which is very relevant in daily life.

By developing mindfulness, knowledge and wisdom grow naturally as the meditator sees HOW things work by witnessing the impersonal process of Dependent Origination.

This leads to a form of happiness the Buddha called Contentment.

Contentment and peacefulness are by-products of living the Buddhist practice.

This meditation also leads to equanimity, balance, and dissolution of fear and other dis-eases.

With less fear and dread the meditator finds new confidence.

Then Loving Kindness, Compassion, Joy, and Equanimity become a part of life.

Letting Go of Craving → The Way to End Suffering)

Craving always manifests as a tension or tightness in both mind and body!

Craving is the start of the "I like it" or "I don't like it" mind.

In other words, craving is the start of the false idea of a personal self (attā).

It's interesting and fun to practice by relaxing the craving and certainly it helps the meditator smile when they see the world around them change in a positive way.

When the meditator is practicing Tranquil Wisdom Insight Meditation, they do not suppress anything.

Suppression means they would push down, push away, or not allow certain types of experiences.

When a hindrance arises, the meditator must work to open their mind by seeing HOW mind's attention moved away from the object of meditation.

The content or story about the distraction doesn't matter at all!

The meditator applies the 6R's, that is, they Recognize, Release, Relax, Re-smile, Return, and Repeat.

Just because a hindrance is let go of doesn't mean that it will go away quickly.

More than likely the disturbance will arise again.

Then the meditator treats it in the same way by practicing the 6R's again.

As the meditator becomes more familiar with this process, they will eventually see that something arose right before mind was carried away and distracted it for a period of time.

The next time the hindrance comes up, the meditator lets go earlier and does the 6R's a little more easily, as mind becomes familiar with this process.

The meditator does this until the hindrance fades away by itself.

At that point, the meditator will have a real sense of relief (pamojja)!

Next they will experience the arising of an intense happiness called joy (pīti).

This joy is a very happy feeling and has a lot of excitement in it.

When the joy fades away the meditator will experience a deep sense of tranquility (passaddhi) and calmness (samādhi).

Following this, there will be a feeling of extreme comfort in both mind and body. This is called happiness in the Buddha's terms.

This is the description of what happens when the meditator attains the first jhāna.

This is clearly seen as anicca (impermanence): this state wasn't there and now it is; dukkha (suffering or un-satisfactoriness): the meditator sees that when these distractions arise they are painful;

and anattā (not taking it personally).

The practitioner begins to see the hindrances more clearly as being an arising impersonal process that the meditator has no control over instead of taking these hindrances as "I am that."

As a result, the meditator begins to see clearly how mind works and this leads to the development of wisdom, which means seeing HOW the impersonal links of Dependent Origination actually occur.

When the meditator allows the hindrances and does not identify with them, they will naturally fade away, and mind's attention will become more clear and bright.

Every time the meditator lets go of the ego attachment of "I am that" (craving), mind naturally becomes more expanded, alert, purified, and radiant.

Thus, one of the main reasons for this book is to show that whenever the meditator suppresses anything, they are not purifying mind, or experiencing things as they truly are.

Any time there is suppression, the meditator is pushing away or not allowing part of their experience and this closes mind instead of expanding and opening mind up.

As a result, such one-pointed concentration is not purifying mind of ignorance or craving.

It is not seeing how mind's attention actually moves by way of the Four Noble Truths.

Therefore, the meditator is actually stopping the process of purification of mind!

It is impossible to experience the unconditioned state of the Supra-mundane Nibbāna if the meditator does not let go of everything that arises.

It is by letting go and relaxing that the meditator purifies mind of the ego belief of "I am that."

The Buddha *never taught suppression of any experience* nor did he teach a meditation that causes mind to fix or to absorb into any meditation object.

Remember, he rejected every form of one-pointed concentration meditation as not being the way that leads to the Cessation of Suffering.

Actually, any kind of pain or emotional upset or physical discomfort and even death should be 6R'd.

It should be accepted through clear understanding with equanimity, full awareness, and soft attention and not personally identified with (attā).

Personality View

Real personality change occurs when the meditator keeps the precepts closely, then opens and expands the mind, let's go of any kind of craving, clinging, hindrances, pain, or suffering and tension even in their daily lives.

This means that the meditator opens and expands their awareness so that they observe everything with a silent mind, which is free from tightness and all false ego-attachment (craving).

When the meditator actually relaxes the tension or tightness in their mind and body, the next thing that will be seen is that mind is bright, alert, clear, and pure!

There are no thoughts to distract the meditator.

There is only the pure observation of a mind free from craving.

This is called the "silent mind," the "eye of wisdom," or as it is sometimes called, "a mind void of craving," which is the Third Noble Truth!

The meditator gradually learns to have a happy and calm life without a lot of mind chatter, especially during their daily activities.

If a meditator practices one-pointed concentration meditation, although they will feel very comfortable and happy while in the deep meditation, when they get out of these exalted stages, their personality and suffering remain the same.

This means that in daily life, when the hindrances attack them, they are not able to clearly recognize, relax, and open their mind to let them go.

Thus, they contract their mind and increase craving by being more attached!

This might even lead to pridefulness and critical mind!

How does this happen?

It is because whenever a hindrance arises during the meditation, the one-pointed concentration meditator lets it go and immediately goes back to the object of meditation again.

They bring back craving to the object of meditation.

This is done without calming and relaxing the tightness caused by the distraction.

Mind tends to close or contract and tighten around that experience (while in sitting meditation) until mind becomes more deeply "concentrated."

As a result, this suppresses the hindrances.

Thus, the meditator has not completely let go of the ego-attachment (attā) to that distraction.

Their mind is also tight and tense because they are not seeing clearly that they are not opening and allowing, but rather they are closing mind's attention tightly and fighting with that distraction.

This explains why nowadays some meditators complain that they have huge amounts of tension in their head and ringing in their ears.

Actually, when the meditator truly let's go of any distraction, there will not ever be any tension in the head or ringing in the ears.

As a result of this tension and tightness during absorption concentration, there is no real purification of mind and thus, stable personality change does not happen very easily.

Now, we are almost ready for the Metta Meditation instructions and the Ānāpānasati Sutta.

But, before we go into that, let's look at some words, which have been changed so that their meanings in the texts become clearer.

For instance, the word "rapture" is replaced by "joy" and the word "pleasure" is changed to "happiness." In addition, the word "concentration" is replaced by "stillness," "collectedness," or "unified mind."

Also, the phrase of "applied and sustained thought" is replaced by "thinking and examining thoughts."

When the meditator practices according to the Buddha's instructions as described here, they will be able to confirm their experiences by reading the suttas.

As a result, there is better understanding of these profound texts.

In these few opening chapters, the author has touched on some controversial views about the practices of absorption or fixed concentration (appaṇā samādhi), access concentration (upacāra samādhi) and momentary concentration (khaṇikha samādhi).

Thus, the author will appreciate it very much, if discrepancies are found, the reader would indicate to him which suttas mention the concentration practices are in doubt.

When the meditator practices Tranquil Wisdom Insight Meditation, there is only opening, expanding of mind, and allowing, then relaxing the tightness caused by the hindrance or distraction.

A smile arises just before going back to the object of meditation again.

This opening and allowing helps the meditator to be more aware and alert to the things which cause pain and suffering, so that the meditator can open up and expand even further.

With this kind of awareness, there is stable personality change and only then can the meditator fulfill the Buddha's admonition of "We are the Happy Ones."

Many people who have been studying the Buddha's Path have approached the author to ask about the added step of smiling, saying "The Buddha never talked about smiling, so, why are you adding this to the Buddhist teachings?"

My simple answer is this: In order to bring up a wholesome state, especially in the west, smiling helps immeasurably to improve mindfulness during the meditator's daily activities and thus a person's sitting practice is better, too!

Smiling helps joy arise and when joy is in the meditator's mind, mind's attention becomes much more alert and agile. This is one of the reasons that Joy is an enlightenment factor.

In the world that we live in today there are not enough happy smiling people.

We can change that.

If we all begin smiling and having contentment as our guide, then, we too can be "The Happy Ones"!

Instructions in Loving-Kindness Meditation

Introduction

Before we start the instructions in the actual practice of loving-kindness meditation it might be helpful to make some preliminary observations.

Loving-Kindness Meditation is not to be practiced by everyone. This is an operational issue and nothing to be taken personally.

The fact is everyone has a definite personality type.

For instance, some types of personality are lustful types. Some are angry personality types, some are dull types of personality, and some are faith types of personality.

If the meditator has a lustful type of personality then the "Loving-kindness Meditation" is not recommended, because they can get caught by their desire and become very attached.

If the person they are sending mettā to gets into an accident, the lustful personality type of person will try to take away their spiritual friends pain by being sad themselves.

For this type of person who has a "lust" personality, it is best for them to do the Mindfulness of Breathing

Meditation, because it helps them to become balanced and more happiness arises in their life.

Again, if the meditator has an angry type of personality, the best meditation for them is the Loving-Kindness Meditation, because this form of meditation will help them to gain balance and happiness in their life.

For example, if a meditator has lots of anger or aversion in their mind, it is not recommended that they do an asubha meditation (foulness of the body meditation). Why?

Because it can cause them to become so depressed and disgusted with their body, they might even consider committing suicide!

This is a very specific meditation and works very well for most people.

Please remember that this is describing an operational process of the meditation, there is nothing personal, and this is not intended to offend anyone.

This type of meditation is not recommended for the meditator who is gay or is bi-sexual.

This is by no means stating that the Buddha was against these kinds of sexual activities, but as far as doing Loving-Kindness Meditation, as a primary meditation, it is just not recommended for gays or bisexuals.

Buddhism is actually an asexual teaching that goes way beyond anything having to do with the sex of an individual.

It has to do with how the Mind of a Human Being actually works.

It is best for those who are gay or bi-sexual to do the Mindfulness of Breathing Meditation. Why?

Because if a gay person chooses to do the Mettā Meditation and they send mettā to a spiritual friend and that is a person of the same sex, then it may cause some unwholesome states of lust to arise or if the meditator picks a person of the opposite sex, it might cause some unwholesome states of hatred to arise.

Either way this is the operational teachings for the meditation on Loving-Kindness and it is not recommended because of the hindrances or problems which may arise and block progress.

There is no finger pointing or condemning here. This is just a statement of fact that helps the meditator to progress more quickly in their meditation practice so that they can become even more happy!

Not every meditation object is suitable for every personality type.

Only the Mindfulness of Breathing, which is a very neutral type of meditation object, works for everyone.

Buddhist meditation is a non-sexual, non-discriminative teaching.

The Buddha looked at different types of meditation objects as tools for balancing the meditators personality and chose the best kind of meditation to suit each type of personality.

The author has included the Loving-Kindness Meditation because for most people this approach works very well and the progress in the meditation is remarkably rapid.

One of the true advantages of doing Mettā Meditation is how quickly the meditator can get into the Jhāna (levels of understanding).

This is not to say that, when the meditator practices Mindfulness of Breathing, the meditator's progress is super slow. It's not.

The mettā seems to be easier to grasp and to do for most people.

The Mettā Meditation is included because many people who come to the meditation center to learn more about meditation have been practicing some form of one-pointed concentration technique in the past.

Many have previously developed habits of using unnecessary levels of concentration while practicing, and it usually is hard for them to remember to add the extra step of relaxing along with what they are already doing.

The guiding teacher has found that, if the student changes their meditation object to Loving-Kindness Meditation, this new kind of practice is so different from what the meditator is used to that it's like starting over again from the beginning.

This learning of a new method will now include the 6R's and this helps the student to change more quickly to this new and wholesome pattern of practice.

This, in turn, helps with their understanding of the Buddha's teachings.

The Mettā Meditation is a tool that will lead the student through all of the Brahma Vihāras, i.e. Metta, Compassion, Unselfish Joy, and Equanimity.

Their understanding of the Four Noble Truths and Dependent Origination becomes deep and clear.

Mettā and the rest of the Brahma Vihāras will guide a student as high as "the Realm of Nothingness."

But, by that time the meditator will wish to continue on and, when they do, they will eventually reach the realm of "Neither-Perception-Nor-Non-Perception."

This is different from the popular belief that mettā is a form of absorption concentration and will only lead the meditator to the 3rd jhāna.

The Mettā Meditation, within the framework of the Brahma Vihāras, actually does lead a meditator to the final goal of Nibbāna just like the practice of Mindfulness of Breathing.

This can be seen if the meditator goes to the Saṃyutta Nikāya, page 1607, "The Enlightenment Factors with Loving-Kindness," by Bhikkhu Bodhi, Wisdom Publications:

This sutta is a very eye-opening discourse.

It says that the practice of Mettā meditation will take the student to the fourth jhāna.

Then it naturally changes to Compassion and "the Realm of Infinite Space." The First Arūpa (Immaterial) Jhāna.

Again, the practice naturally changes to Unselfish Joy and "the Realm of Infinite Consciousness." The Second Arūpa (immaterial) Jhāna.

It naturally changes once more to equanimity and "the Realm of Nothingness." The Third Arūpa (immaterial) Jhāna.

By that time, the meditator is committed to seeing it through, continuing to practice their 6R's, and they will eventually reach the realm of "Neither Perception nor Non-perception" (neither feeling nor non-feeling; neither consciousness nor non-consciousness). The Fourth Arūpa (immaterial) jhāna.

From there the meditator will experience cessation (nirodha) and attain the goal of Nibbāna!

The Mettā Meditation includes the Four Foundations of Mindfulness, the Four Spiritual Powers, the Four Kinds of Right Striving, the Five Faculties, the Five Powers, the Seven Enlightenment Factors, and the Eight-Fold Path.

The meditator will learn these Thirty-Seven Requisites of Enlightenment through direct experience, when they practice either the Mindfulness of Metta or the Mindfulness of Breathing meditation.

Understanding and experiencing all of the above mentioned factors are necessary in order to attain Nibbāna.

They need to be practiced while the meditator is in each of the jhānas or levels of understanding.

With all of this said, let us go to the instructions for this practice.

Mettā Meditation Instructions

When practicing Loving-Kindness Meditation, you first start by sending loving and kind thoughts to yourself.

Begin by remembering a time when you were happy.

Remember your first pet or a time you first held a puppy and you were so happy and loved that puppy so much.

Or remember any other time that this feeling of love was so strong and you were happy!

When the feeling of happiness arises, it is a warm glowing feeling radiating from the center of your chest.

When this feeling arises, make a very sincere wish for your own happiness, "May I be happy," "May I be filled with joy," "May I be peaceful and calm," "May I be cheerful and kind."

Make a sincere wish that not only helps the person you are radiating to but helps yourself as well!

The wish can be for a clear, accepting mind.

Then, **feel** that wish and place it in your heart and radiate it.

The wish can be for an open happy mind.

Again, **feel** that openness and happiness and radiate that wish from your heart.

Whatever wish you make, please **feel** that wish in yourself before radiating it out to another person.

This is important! The meditator must **feel** the wish first before giving it away.

If the meditator doesn't feel the wish, how can they give it to someone else?

Make it sincere and something that comes directly from your heart!

Make any wholesome, sincere wish that has meaning for you; put the feeling of that sincere wish in your heart.

The key word here is "**sincere**." If your wish isn't a sincere wish, then it will turn into a mantra; that is, it may become a statement repeated by rote, with no real meaning.

Repeating of the same insincere wish turns out not to be sincere and it will slow down the meditator's progress.

When using a sincere wish, if the meditator wants to make the same wish over and over again, as long as that wish has real meaning for you, then do that.

Ultimately it is up to you personally what wish is made.

When the meditator makes the wish by rote, mind is only on the surface, repeating the statement while thinking about other things.

This means that the meditator isn't actually meditating at that time, they are being caught by restlessness and this hindrance absolutely stops any progress at all.

If the meditator recognizes that this is happening then they must 6R it and, with a slight smile, start over with a different wish.

It is very important that the wish the meditator makes for oneself (and later for their spiritual friend) has real meaning and uses their whole undivided attention.

DO NOT continually repeat the wish for happiness: "May I be happy... may I be happy... may I be happy... may I be happy."

Make the wish sincerely for your own happiness when the feeling of Loving-Kindness begins to fade a little.

Relaxing Tension

The following is a very important part of the meditation instruction:

After every wish for your own happiness, please notice that there is some slight tension or tightness in your head, in your mind.

6R the tension, let it go, relax that tightness from the mental verbalization, then smile and continue. **Please let go of this only one time!**

If the tightness doesn't go away—never mind, you will be able to use the 6R's and let it go while on the meditation object (your home base).

Don't continually try to keep relaxing mind, without coming back to the home base; always softly redirect your tranquil attention back to the feeling of happiness and radiate that feeling.

How to Sit

When you sit in meditation please *do not move your body, at all.*

Sit with your back nicely straight, but not rigid.

Try to have every vertebra stacked comfortably one on top of the other.

This position has the tendency to bring your chest up a little, so that it can be easier to radiate the feeling of love.

Sit with your legs in a comfortable position.

If you cross them too tightly the circulation in your legs may stop, causing your legs to go to sleep, and this becomes very painful.

If you need to sit on a cushion, or in a chair, that's okay.

Choose a posture that doesn't bring up pain.

If you sit in a chair, however, please don't lean heavily back into it. Leaning back can stop the energy flow up your back and can make you feel sleepy.

To help this situation, please place a rolled towel at the bottom of your back between you and the chair. This will help you sit towards the front of the chair and allow for proper energy flow.

Just sit in a comfortable way.

Please *don't move your body for any reason at all* while sitting.

Don't wiggle your toes; don't wiggle your fingers; don't scratch; don't rub; don't rock your body; don't change your posture at all.

In fact, if you can sit as still as a Buddha image, this would be the best!

If you move around, it becomes a big distraction to your practice and you won't progress very quickly, if at all.

While you are sitting, radiating the warm glowing feeling of Loving-Kindness in the center of your chest and making a sincere wish, feeling that wish in your heart, your mind will wander away and begin to think about other things.

This is normal.

How to Do the Walking Meditation

One thing to observe before we go to the walking meditation is:

The walking meditation is a very important part of the training and needs to be practiced!!!

Please do not change your posture, because the body wants to be relieved from some discomfort, and then continue doing the sitting meditation.

The meditator is learning a few things from this part of the practice and it has to do with learning to be mindful in one's daily life as well as getting exercise for the body.

When it's time for the sitting to change position, after sitting for no less than 30 minutes, then do the walking meditation.

The meditator stays with the object of meditation, i.e. the breath and relaxing, or the mettā and relaxing and doesn't change to focusing on the body movements.

Please don't place mind's attention on the feet while walking, or begin walking very slowly.

If the mind's attention is on the feet, the meditator is not very aware of what mind's attention is doing.

Why? Because the meditator is not watching what mind's attention is doing and they are trying to over-focus on just the movements of the feet.

The question that needs to be asked here is: "Is the meditator being truly mindful of HOW mind's attention moves from one thing to another, when over-focusing on only the movement of the feet?"

The meditator needs to walk at a regular pace just as they do when walking from one place to another in their normal life!

There are some real advantages to walking this way, because the blood starts moving around better and one's body gets some exercise, so muscles can stretch out and let any stiffness go.

Walking in a normal to fast pace also energizes one's body, so sloth or torpor won't become as much of a problem.

When the meditator is doing walking meditation, they need to keep their eyes down, not be looking around.

Why? Because where the eyes go, so goes mind's attention.

Before too long, mind is thinking this or that and is completely distracted and not aware of the object of meditation

The meditator stays on the breath and relaxing, or, mettā and relaxing, using the 6R's whenever mind's attention gets distracted.

At first, mind's attention will be somewhat active and lots of wandering thoughts will invade it.

But, with calm patience in 6R-ing, those distractions will eventually settle down and the meditator will be able to stay with their object of meditation.

Eventually, the walking meditation will become as good as the sitting meditation.

This way, when one is off of retreat they can bring their meditation into their daily activities more easily.

It is recommended that the student walk fast enough so that the heart beats a little more quickly and that they continue for at least 15 minutes.

When the meditation is good, they can walk for longer but not more than 45 minutes or the body can become tired.

How to Handle Wandering Thoughts

The Buddha's advice to us was "not to Crave or Cling to anything!"

It's really important to understand that "Thoughts are never your enemy to fight with"!

Please don't fight with them, try to push them away, or try to control them in any way.

When a series of thoughts arises and takes mind's attention away, notice that you are not experiencing the feeling of Loving-Kindness and making a wish for your own happiness.

Then, simply 6R (let go of) the thought.

The content of any thought is not important at all!

Being able to see HOW mind's attention got distracted is important because this is the way you teach yourself how Dependent Origination actually occurs!

> Let go of all thoughts no matter how interesting or "important" they may seem at the time.
>
> Even if you are in mid-sentence, just 6R it.
>
> Let go of the thought, let it be there by itself without keeping your attention on it.
>
> This is done by not continuing to think the thought, no matter how important it seems at that time.

At this point, there is another very important step:

> Notice the tightness or tension in your head and mind.

There is a membrane wrapped around the brain and every time a thought, sensation, or a feeling arises, this membrane contracts and gets tight.

This tightness or tension is how the meditator can recognize craving when it arises!

This important step of relaxing shows you how to let go of Craving, which if done correctly demonstrates the Cessation of Suffering the Buddha talked about.

> As you Relax, feel the tightness open and mind become clear.
>
> Mind feels as if it expands and relaxes.
>
> It then becomes very tranquil and calm.
>
> At this time there are no thoughts, and mind is exceptionally clear and alert.
>
> Immediately, bring that clear mind back to your object of meditation, that is, the feeling of Loving-Kindness and making a sincere wish for your own happiness.

It doesn't matter how many times mind's attention goes away and thinks about other things.

What really matters is that you see that mind's attention has become distracted by a thought and how that attention has moved away from the mettā, smiling, and relaxing.

The same method holds true for any sensation or emotional feeling that pulls mind's attention to it.

6R it by recognizing mind's distraction and movement away from Loving-Kindness, release it, relax, re-smile, return, and repeat and staying with the mettā.

Please remember to "roll your R's," not repeat each step individually in your mind. This needs to develop into a flowing type of motion.

Strengthen Awareness: Every time you 6R and let go of a distraction or make a wish for your happiness, relax the tightness caused by the movement of mind's attention, and redirect your tranquil attention back to the feeling of being happy and smiling, you are strengthening your mindfulness (observation power).

Therefore, please don't criticize yourself because you think that you "should" do better, or that your thoughts, sensations, and emotional feelings are the enemy to be squashed and destroyed.

These kinds of critical, hard-hearted thoughts and feelings contain aversion, and aversion is the opposite of the practice of Loving-Acceptance.

Loving-Kindness and Loving-Acceptance are different words that say basically the same thing.

So, please be kind to yourself and smile!

Make this a fun kind of game to play with, not an enemy to fight with.

The importance of relaxing the tightness or tension after every arising thought, sensation, or emotional feeling can't be overstated.

When you let go of this tightness you are letting go of "craving."

It is very important to understand this because craving is the cause of all suffering.

Craving and Ego-Identification

Craving always manifests as tightness or tension in your head/mind.

It is identified as the "I like it" or "I don't like it" mind and is the first sign of the wrong idea of the I/ME/MINE belief.

When you let go of tightness, what you are actually doing is letting go of craving and the false idea of "a personal self" or "ego identification."

This is how you purify mind's attention and become happier and more uplifted, all of the time.

While you are sitting still, there may be some sensations that arise in your body.

You may feel an itch, heat, tension, a feeling of coughing, wanting to sneeze, or a pain.

Please don't move your body for any reason at all.

When such a feeling arises, mind's attention will immediately go to that feeling.

Let's say an itch or cough.

Mind's attention moves to the distraction by itself.

The first thing that mind does is it begins to think about the feeling:

"I wish this would go away" ... "I want this to stop bothering me" ... "I hate this feeling" ... "Why doesn't it just go away" ... "I want this to stop."

Every time you entertain these kinds of thoughts, the sensation becomes bigger and more intense.

It actually turns into an emergency in your mind.

Then, you won't be able to stand it anymore, and you feel like you have to move to relieve that discomfort.

But the instructions are: *don't move your body for any reason at all*.

Instead, watch the movements of mind's attention.

So, what can we do about this?

We need to open up and allow the feeling to be there:

> Open up: First, notice that your mind has become distracted by the itch or cough, etc., and the thoughts about that sensation.
>
> Now, let go of those thoughts, simply let them be.
>
> Next notice the tightness in your head/mind and relax.
>
> Every time a sensation (or emotional feeling) arises, it is only natural for mind to make a tight fist around it.
>
> This tight mental fist is aversion.
>
> Open up and allow the itch (or emotional feeling) to be there.
>
> Remember that it is okay if the tightness doesn't go away immediately.

The "Truth (Dhamma) of the present moment" is that when an itch or any other sensation arises, it is there!

What you do with this Dhamma dictates whether you will suffer more unnecessarily or not.

Resisting the itch and trying to think it away produces both more subtle and gross pain.

Five Aggregates

We have five different things that make up this mind/body process.

They are called the Five Aggregates affected by craving and clinging.

They are: Physical Body (rūpa), Feeling (vedanā), Perception (saññā), Thoughts (saṅkhāra), and Consciousness (viññāṇa).

As you can see, feeling[1], is one thing and thoughts are another.

If we try to control our feeling with our thoughts, the resistance that you have to a feeling causes it to get bigger and more intense.

In fact, it becomes so big that it turns into a true emergency (real un-satisfactoriness - Dukkha).

Then you can't stand the sensation (or emotional feeling) anymore.

You feel that you have to move.

While you are sitting in meditation, if you move your body even a little bit, it breaks the continuity of practice and you have to start over again.

Letting go of the thoughts about the sensation or emotional feeling means that you are letting go of the want to control the feeling with your thoughts.

It also means that you are letting go of "craving," which directly leads to the Cessation of Suffering.

Next, you notice the tight mental fist around the sensation, and let go of that aversion to it.

Simply allow the itch or cough (sensation or emotional feeling) to be there by itself.

See it as if it were a bubble floating in the air; the bubble floats freely.

Whichever way the wind blows, the bubble will float in that direction.

If the wind changes and blows in another direction, the bubble goes in that direction without any resistance at all

> This practice is learning how to lovingly-accept whatever arises in the present moment.

> Now again, notice that subtle tightness or tension in your head/mind, relax, re-smile, and softly redirect your gentle loving attention back to the feeling of radiating love from your heart and making a wish for your own happiness.

The true nature of these kinds of sensations (and emotional feelings) is that they don't go away right away.

Mind's attention will bounce back and forth from your object of meditation (that is radiating the feeling of love and making a sincere wish for your happiness) to that feeling.

Every time this happens you treat it in the same way:

- **Know:** Know or recognize when mind's attention has become distracted.
- **Let go:** Let it be there without getting involved with the content of any thoughts, sensations or emotional feelings.

- **Relax:** Relax the tightness, let go of the tight mental fist around the feeling, let it be there by itself.
- **Smile:** bring up the wholesome and lightly smile, so that mind's attention can be more alert, uplifted, and happy!
- **Come back:** Come back to your object of meditation with mind's attention - light and craving-free. That is radiating the feeling of love and making a sincere wish for your happiness and feeling that wish in your heart.
- **Continue:** Continue to stay with the object of meditation until mindfulness slips again. Then start this whole process again!

How to Radiate Love

Remember, it's O.K. for that thought, sensation, or emotional feeling to be there, because that is the truth of the present moment.

An acronym that works very well to help as a reminder is, **"DROPSS."**

"Don't Resist or Push - Soften and SMILE."

Allow the thought, sensation, or emotional feeling to be, without trying to make it be anything other than it is.

Relax the subtle (and sometimes not so subtle) tightness or tension in your head/mind, and gently redirect your tranquil attention back to your meditation object.

After doing this for about 10 minutes, then begin sending loving and kind thoughts to your spiritual friend.

A spiritual friend is someone who, when you think of them and their good qualities, it makes you happy.

This is a friend who is of the same sex, they are alive, and not a member of your family.

This is for right now.

Later, you will be able to send Loving-Kindness to all of the members of your family.

But, for this training period, please choose another friend.

Once you start sending Loving-Kindness to your spiritual friend, please don't change to another person.

Stay with your same spiritual friend until you get to the third or fourth meditation level of understanding (Jhāna).

As you are sending a sincere wish for your own happiness, then mentally you say:

"As I wish this feeling of peace and calm (happiness, joy, whatever) for myself, I wish this feeling for you, too." "May you be well, happy, and peaceful."

Then start radiating this feeling of love and peace to your friend.

It is quite important for you to feel the sincere wish and that you place that feeling in your heart before you send it out.

Visualization

The meditator should also visualize the spiritual friend in your mind's eye.

For example, you can visualize your friend as you remember them in a photograph or as you have seen them moving around in a home movie.

The exact visualization doesn't matter.

But when you see your friend, see him or her smiling and happy.

This can help to remind you to be smiling and happy, too!

The visualization can be somewhat difficult.

It can sometimes be cloudy or fuzzy, or a long distance away, or it can be there for just a moment and disappear. That is all right.

Don't try too hard, because it will give you a headache.

Some people can't see the visualization at all, so it's all right to bring your friend into your heart by using their name.

The meditator wants about 75% of the time spent on the feeling of Loving-Kindness,

20% (more or less, depending on what is happening) on making a sincere wish and feeling that wish in your heart; this helps the feeling for your friend's happiness to grow.

Only about 5% of your time should be spent on visualizing your friend.

By this, you can see that the "Feeling and radiating Loving-Kindness" is by far the most important part of the meditation, and, the visualization is the least important part.

But still put a little effort into the visualization.

Eventually it will get better and easier.

Smiling

This is a smiling meditation!

While you are sitting and radiating love to your spiritual friend (or to yourself), smile with your mind.

Even though your eyes are closed during the meditation, smile with your eyes.

This helps to let go of tension in your face.

Put a little smile on your lips and put a smile in your heart.

Smiling is nice and most helpful to practice all of the time, but especially when you are sitting in meditation.

The more we can learn to smile the happier mind becomes.

It may sound a little silly, but scientists have discovered that the corners of our mouth are very important; the position of the lips corresponds to different mental states.

When the corners of your lips turn down, your thoughts tend to become heavy and unwholesome.

When the corners of your lips go up, mind becomes more uplifted and clear, so joy can arise more often.

This is important to remember, because a smile can help you to change your perspective about all kinds of feelings and thoughts.

Please, try to remember to smile into everything that arises and everything that you direct your mind's attention to.

In other words, smile as much as you can into everything all day long.

Dullness of Mind

The more sincere and enthusiastic you are in sending Loving-Kindness to yourself and your spiritual friend, the less you will experience sleepiness or dullness of mind.

When sleepiness or dullness occurs, your body may begin to slump.

This is the only time that you can move your body and straighten up.

But don't do this too often either.

If you see mind's attention starting to dull out, then take more interest in your friend; see him or her doing things that you truly appreciate.

For example, you can visualize times when they were helpful and generous, or times when they made you happy and you laughed with them.

This can help to increase your interest and energy, and then the dullness will subside.

Once you begin this meditation, please start by sitting for no less than half an hour.

The first ten minutes you send Loving-Kindness to yourself.

The rest of the time, send love to your spiritual friend (remember the same friend all of the time).

When your meditation becomes better and you feel more comfortable, you can sit for a longer period of time (whatever is appropriate for you with your time constraints).

But don't sit for less than thirty minutes a day in the beginning! More if you have the time.

Active Meditation

This is not simply a passive meditation to be practiced only when you are sitting in a chair or on a cushion.

It's a meditation to be practiced all of the time, especially when you do your daily activities.

So many times we walk around in a mental haze of random nonsense thoughts.

Why not try practicing Loving-Kindness Meditation whenever we can possibly remember?

When you are walking from your house to your car or from your car to your job, what is your mind doing? Ho hum; probably more nonsense thoughts.

This is the time to notice what your mind is doing in the present moment and let go of these distracting thoughts.

Relax the tightness in your head/mind and wish someone happiness!

It doesn't matter whom you send loving thoughts and feelings to in your daily activities.

It can be to the person walking next to you, your spiritual friend, yourself, or all beings.

The key words here are to "send love," smiling and feeling that sincere wish.

Do this as much as possible during the day.

The more we focus on sending and radiating loving and kind thoughts, the more we affect the world around us in a positive way.

As a result, your mind becomes uplifted and happy at the same time. Nice!

Benefits of Loving-Kindness

There are many benefits to practicing Loving-Kindness:

You go to sleep easily and sleep soundly.

When you wake up, you wake easily and quickly and you are not groggy anymore.

Heavenly beings will guard and protect you.

People and animals like you.

Your face becomes radiant and beautiful, when you practice Loving-Kindness.

Your mind becomes collected more quickly than with any other type of meditation.

Actually, the Buddha mentioned Mindfulness of Loving-Kindness Meditation and the Four Brahma Vihāras (Loving-Kindness, Compassion, Unselfish Joy, and Equanimity) more times than he did Mindfulness of Breathing Meditation.

You can see just how important the Buddha thought it was.

Loving Kindness and Nibbāna

The practice of Loving-Kindness Meditation can lead you directly to the experience of Nibbāna if you follow all of the Brahma Vihāras:

that is, the practice of Loving- Kindness, Compassion, Unselfish Joy, and Equanimity.

This is mentioned many times in the suttas (the original discourses of the Buddha).

Many times other teachers will say that this practice alone doesn't directly lead the meditator to the experience of Nibbāna.

This is true.

But, when Loving-Kindness Meditation is practiced as part of the Brahma Vihāras, then it will take the meditator to the fourth Jhāna or meditation level.

This is where the Buddha tried to have all of the students who practiced meditation get to.

The fourth meditation level is where the meditator experiences deep states of equanimity.

According to the suttas, there are three different paths that can be taken once the meditator reaches this level.

These paths can take the meditator directly to the experience of Nibbāna.

We will not go into more detail at this time, because it may cause some confusion.

But if you are interested in having more information, please start reading suttas like sutta #62, "The Mahārchulovada Sutta" in the Middle Length Discourses of the Buddha.

Or you can read sutta #27 "The Culahatthipadopama Sutta" in the same book.

I sincerely hope that these meditation instructions are helpful to you and that by practicing in this way you will benefit greatly and lead a truly happy and healthy life.

The Ānāpānasati Sutta

Majjhima Nikāya

(Middle Length Discourses)

Introduction

1] Thus have I heard. On one occasion the Blessed One was living at Sāvatthī in the Eastern Park, in the Palace of Migara's Mother, together with many very well-known elder disciples –

– the Venerable Sāriputta, the Venerable Mahā -Moggallāna, the Venerable Mahā Kassapa, the Venerable Mahā Kaccana, the Venerable Mahā Kotthita, the Venerable Mahā Kappina, the Venerable Cunda, the Venerable Anaruddha, the Venerable Revata, the Venerable Ananda, and other very well-known elder disciples.

2] Now on that occasion elder Monks had been teaching and instructing new monks;

some elder monks had been teaching and instructing ten new monks,

some elder monks had been teaching and instructing twenty new monks,

some elder monks had been teaching and instructing thirty new monks,

some elder monks had been teaching and instructing forty new monks.

And the new monks, taught and instructed by the elder monks, had achieved successive stages of high distinction.

*3] On that occasion - the Uposatha day of
the fifteenth, on the full-moon night of the
Pavāraṇā ceremony - the Blessed One was
seated in the open surrounded by the Sangha
of monks.*

*Then, surveying the silent Sangha of monks,
he addressed them thus:*

4] Monks, I am content with this progress.

My mind is content with this progress.

*So arouse still more energy to attain the
unattained, to achieve the unachieved, to
realize the unrealized.*

*I shall wait here at Sāvatthī for the Komudi
full moon of the fourth month.*

The monks can still practice their meditation or make new
robes and prepare to go out wandering or teaching the
Dhamma to other monks and laypersons during this extra
month.

The Kathina Ceremony is also held during this month.

This is the time for lay men and lay women to make extra
merit by practicing their generosity by giving robes and
other requisites to the Sangha members.

5] The monks of the countryside heard:

*"The Blessed One will wait there at Sāvatthī
for the Komudi full moon of the fourth
month."*

And the monks of the countryside left in due course for Sāvatthī to see the Blessed One.

6] And the elder monks still more intensively taught and instructed new monks;

some elder monks taught and instructed ten new monks,

some elder monks taught and instructed twenty new monks,

some elder monks taught and instructed thirty new monks,

some elder monks taught and instructed forty new monks.

And the new monks, taught and instructed by the elder monks, achieved successive stages of high distinction.

7] On that occasion - the Uposatha day of the fifteenth, the full-moon night of the Komudi full moon of the fourth month - the Blessed One was seated in the open surrounded by the Sangha of monks.

Then, surveying the silent Sangha of monks, he addressed them thus:

8] "Monks, this assembly is free from prattle;

this assembly is free from chatter. [10]

It consists purely of heartwood.

*Such is this Sangha of Monks; such is this
assembly.*

*Such an assembly as is worthy of gifts,
worthy of hospitality, worthy of offerings,
worthy of reverential salutation, an
incomparable field of merit for the world –
Such is this assembly.*

*Such an assembly that a small gift given to it
becomes great and a great gift becomes
greater - such is this Sangha of Monks -
such is this assembly.*

*Such an assembly as is rare for the world to
see - such is this Saṅgha of Monks; such is
this assembly.*

*Such an assembly as would be worthy
journeying many leagues with a travel-bag to
see - such is this Saṅgha of Monks; such is
this assembly.*

*9] "In this Saṅgha of Monks, there are monks
who are arahats with taints destroyed, who
have lived the holy life, done what had to be
done, laid down the burden, reached the true
goal, destroyed the fetters of being, and are
completely liberated through final knowledge –
such monks are there in this Saṅgha of
Monks.*

This is the stage where all of the fetters are destroyed, such
that they will not even arise anymore. The ten fetters are:

1. Belief in a permanent self or soul, (Sakkāyadiṭṭhi)

2. Doubt in the correct path, (Vicikiccha,)
3. Belief that chanting, or rites and rituals lead one to Nibbāna, (Sīlabbataparāmāsa)
4. Lust or greed, (Kāmarāga)
5. Hatred or aversion, (Paṭigha)
6. Greed for fine-material existence (Rūparāga) or immaterial existence (Arūparāga)
7. Conceit or pride, (Mana)
8. Sloth and torpor - dullness of mind, (Middha)
9. Restlessness or agitation of mind, (Uddhacca)
10. Ignorance (avijjā)

The final stage of Arahats is described as follows:

They are the ones who have lived the Holy Life, laid down the burden, reached the true goal, destroyed the fetters of being, and are completely liberated through final knowledge, they have done their work with diligence; they are no longer capable of being negligent.

(Taken from the Majjhima Nikāya sutta number 70 section 12.)

Ānāpānasati Sutta- Section 10

10] In this Saṅgha of Monks there are monks who, with the destruction of the five lower fetters, are due to reappear spontaneously (in the pure abodes) and there attain final Nibbāna, without ever returning from that world - such monks are there in this Saṅgha of Monks.

This stage of sainthood is called Anāgāmī where lust and hate no longer even arise in one's mind.

The five lower fetters have been destroyed, but there is still work to be done.

> *11] In this Saṅgha of Monks there are monks who, with the destruction of three fetters and with the attenuation of lust, hate and delusion, are once-returners, returning once to this world to make an end of suffering - such monks are there in this Saṅgha of Monks.*

This stage of sainthood is called being a Sakadāgāmī or once-returner.

They have given up the belief in a permanent self, belief that one can attain enlightenment by chanting and practicing rites and rituals, and they have given up doubt in the path.

Also, the person who has attained this stage has tremendously weakened lust and hatred, together with all of the other fetters.

> *12] In this Saṅgha of Monks there are monks who, with the destruction of the three fetters, are stream-enterers, no longer subject to perdition, bound [for deliverance], headed for enlightenment - such monks are there in this Saṅgha of Monks.*

The person who has attained this stage of enlightenment is called a Sotāpanna or stream-enterer.

They have given up the three lower fetters mentioned above; they are never going to be reborn in a low existence again.

Their lowest rebirth will be as a human being, and the most lifetimes that they will experience before attaining final Nibbāna, is seven.

13] In this Saṅgha of Monks there are monks who abide devoted to the development of the four foundations of mindfulness [11] –such monks are there in this Saṅgha of Monks.

In this Saṅgha of Monks there are monks who abide devoted to the four right kinds of strivings (efforts) - such monks are there in this Saṅgha of Monks.

In this Saṅgha of Monks there are monks who abide devoted to the four bases for spiritual power - such monks are there in this Saṅgha of Monks.

In this Saṅgha of Monks there are monks who abide devoted to the five faculties - such monks are there in this Saṅgha of Monks.

In this Saṅgha of Monks there are monks who abide devoted to the five powers - such monks are there in this Saṅgha of Monks.

In this Saṅgha of Monks there are monks who abide devoted to the seven awakening factors - such monks are there in this Saṅgha of Monks.

In this Saṅgha of Monks there are monks who abide devoted to the Noble Eightfold Path - such monks are there in this Saṅgha of Monks

This list is commonly called the Thirty-Seven Requisites of Awakening.

That is:

The Four Foundations of Mindfulness
The Four Right Kinds of Effort
The Four Bases for Spiritual Power
The Five Faculties
The Five Powers
The Seven Awakening Factors
The Noble Eight-Fold Path

These thirty-seven are described in (Greater Discourse to Sakuludayin) Mahāsakuludayi Sutta # 77, Section 16 of the Majjhima Nikāya, as ways to develop wholesome states.

This sutta describes the qualities of Lord Buddha, demonstrating how his disciples honor, respect, revere and venerate him and live in dependence on him.

We will now look into the meanings of these terms.

The Four Foundations of Mindfulness, the Seven Awakening Factors and the Noble Eightfold Path will be discussed later.

The Four Right Kinds of Effort

Again Udāyin, I have proclaimed to my disciples the way to develop the four right kinds of effort. A monk awakens enthusiasm, for the non-arising of unarisen evil unwholesome states, and he makes effort, arouses energy, exerts his mind, and strives.

Besides enthusiasm, the Pāli word *"chanda"* also means joyful or wholesome interest or enthusiasm.

This kind of desire is wholesome because there is no craving in mind at that time.

A mind which points towards a wholesome object like joy has this quality of joyful interest.

Thus, the first right kind of effort is to cultivate a mind that has joyful interest and enthusiasm, so that mind becomes clear and free from unwholesome states.

Joy grows when mind is smiling and happy during our daily life as well as during sitting meditation.

As a result, mind will be uplifted and wholesome at that time.

Nowadays, these four kinds of effort are usually called the four right efforts.

Some meditation teachers request the meditator to put out strenuous effort to note what is happening in the present moment.

But the sutta here clearly shows that this is not the kind of effort that is being referred to here.

Mindfulness of joyful interest and enthusiasm, i.e., having a smiling mind leads to a light, open, accepting mind without any tension.

This is the proper definition of right effort and, according to the sutta, it actually has nothing to do with noting phenomena until it goes away.

> *He awakens enthusiasm for the abandoning of arisen evil unwholesome states, and he makes effort, arouses energy, exerts his mind, and strives.*

The second right kind of effort teaches one to abandon heavy emotional states like anger, sadness, jealousy, anxiety, stress, panic, depression, fear, etc., and replace them with a smiling mind, which relaxes away even the subtlest tension.

This is the wholesome state of joyful interest and enthusiasm.

By cultivating such a smiling mind, one overcomes the ego-identification with these states as being I/Me/Mine.

A good sense of humor about oneself is a skillful tool to develop when journeying down the spiritual path.

He awakens enthusiasm for the arising of unarisen wholesome states, and he makes effort, arouses energy, exerts his mind, and strives.

This means seeing that mind brings up joyful interest and enthusiasm when these wholesome states are not in mind.

In other words, the cultivation of mindfulness means cultivating joy and a smiling mind.

Even when there is a neutral mind that is merely thinking this and that, this is the time to practice smiling in mind and experiencing joyful interest and enthusiasm.

He awakens enthusiasm for the continuous, non-disappearance, strengthening, increase, and fulfillment by development of arisen wholesome states, and he makes effort, arouses energy, exerts his mind, and strives. And thereby many disciples of mine abide having reached the consummation and perfection of direct knowledge.

The fourth right kind of effort refers to a continuous practice, not only during the formal practice of meditation, but also during our daily activities.

This Right Striving is what is called the 6R's and it needs to be continually practiced when the meditator is doing their sitting practice and when the meditator is performing daily activities.

At one time, some students approached the author and asked:

"How can one attain Nibbāna by practicing smiling and having joyful interest?"

They thought that they had made a very profound statement, because they had been told that only looking at pain and suffering all of the time would help them to attain Nibbāna.

These students are not practicing how to be light and happy as taught by the Lord Buddha.

The author replied to them by asking some cross-questions:

1. "How can you get to Nibbāna without smiling and having joyful interest in your mind?"
2. "Isn't joy one of the awakening factors?"
3. "Didn't the Lord Buddha say, 'We are the Happy Ones'?"
4. "Don't we have to follow the Buddha's instructions to have a wholesome uplifted mind?"
5. "Can a meditator have an uplifted mind without joy?"

Here one realizes the importance of developing a mind that smiles and has joyful interest in how that mind operates.

When they have a joyful interest in how mind works and they have a smile, one is not so heavy and grumpy when things become difficult and there arises a true change of perspective towards life in general.

This is because there is not so much ego-attachment (attā) and the meditator begins to see situations in life more clearly.

When mind does not smile and has no joyful interest, everything becomes heavy and all mental states and thoughts become depressing.

Mind becomes over serious and has lots of craving in it (tension and tightness) and takes everything unclearly, very personally and negatively.

For example, let's say that you are very happy and I come along and give you a rose.

You might take that rose and admire the color, the shape, and the fragrance.

You think, "What a beautiful flower! Just seeing it makes me even happier."

But, if you are in a depressing or angry mood and I come along and give you that same rose, your mind would see the thorns instead.

You might even think, "Ugh! This rose is so ugly. I hate it!"

At that time, all that is seen is the thorns.

But, in actual fact, the rose is the same.

The only difference is your perspective.

Joyful interest and smiling helps to make the world around you a better place to live.

However, this is not to say that we won't go through trials and tribulations.

With practice the meditator will change their perspective to wholesomeness of joy in mind and this changes a big insurmountable problem into a small bump in the road.

This is the magic of having joy arise by using Right Striving to shift our perspective.!

The Four Bases for Spiritual Power

Again, Udāyin, I have proclaimed to my disciples the way to develop the four bases for spiritual power. Here a monk develops the basis for spiritual power consisting of collectedness due to enthusiasm and determined effort.

The first "spiritual power" refers to **enthusiasm** and wholesome desire. It is pointing mind's attention to dwell on something without any craving in it.

In Pāli this is called "Chanda."

Wholesome desire (chanda) means that mind's attention is softly directed to smile and to stay on the object of meditation as much as possible with true enthusiasm.

When the meditator begins to see HOW Dependent Origination and the Four Noble Truths actually work, they gain confidence that they are truly progressing along the path to awakening!

These discoveries help the meditator to have a real sense of fun when meditating.

It keeps one's curiosity going and prompts the question, "I wonder what will happen next," or as Venerable Suzuki Roshi called this, "beginner's mind."

This is opposed to "I have seen this before and I know what comes next."

When this is achieved the meditator begins to see real progress in meditation and then everything in life becomes a part of this practice and in this way mind becomes more open and ready to learn all the Dhamma that the Buddha has to give us.

> *He develops the basis for spiritual power consisting of collectedness due to energy, and determined effort.*

The development of **energy** is very interesting, because this needs to be done often by the sincere meditator.

When the meditator's mindfulness is sharp, they will easily notice when their energy becomes sluggish and mind's attention slips off of the meditation object.

Of course, this is when sloth and torpor take over and the meditator's mind becomes very tired and sleepy.

Also, when one's energy becomes too strong and restlessness sets in, the meditator's mind becomes agitated by thoughts about things.

The thing is, energy has to be monitored fairly often.

The meditator learns to recognize how the energy changes and how to adjust the amount of energy used to stay on the object of meditation in a balanced way.

When the meditator begins to get into the Arūpa Jhānas, this skill becomes very necessary in order to stay in a particular realm with the proper balance of mind, adjusting slightly one way or the other, so that mind's attention remains sharp and alert.

This is another way the hindrances help one to learn just how tricky mind can be and they teach the meditator HOW craving arises.

> **He develops the basis for spiritual power consisting in collectedness due to** purity of mind, **and determined effort.**

The third spiritual power is learning how to develop true **"purity of mind."**

This means that the meditator needs to practice the 6R's every time mind's attention becomes distracted. Why?

Because when one uses the 6R's in a fluid and smooth way, they are letting go of the tension or tightness caused by craving and purifying mind!

When mind's attention has no craving in it, it is considered by the Buddha to be completely pure and free from attachment.

When the meditator lets go of craving, mind has no thoughts in it and mind's attention is exceedingly bright, clear and alert.

The Buddha referred to this kind of attention as seeing with the "Eyes of Wisdom."

This type of mind is considered to be void of any hindrances at all.

It is void of distractions and void of the belief in a personal self (attā).

This is true voidness as described deeply by the Buddha in sutta # 121, Section 4, "The Shorter Discourse on Voidness," Majjhima Nikāya. It says:

*Thus he regards it as void of what is not
there, but as to what remains there he
understands that which is present thus: 'This
is present.'*

*Thus, Ānanda, this is his genuine,
undistorted, pure descent into voidness.*

**He develops the basis for spiritual power
consisting of collectedness due to investigation,
and determined effort.**

The fourth spiritual power is learning how to develop the
Buddha's form of **investigation.**

Remember, meditation is not about thinking or analyzing
anything, but meditation is about expanding the meditator's
awareness of HOW mind's attention stays in the present
moment and then going beyond that, to the true expression
of loving acceptance.

Meditation is the silence when thoughts, with all their
images and words, have entirely ceased.

It is a mind free from craving, watching carefully how
things work with the "eye of wisdom," that is, the truly
observant and alert mind.

How to Purify Mind

This form of meditation turns out to be about a gentle
collectedness and full awareness instead of a process of
one-pointed concentration.

Whereas, **an improperly developed mind** using
absorption concentration:

- creates a tension and tightness of mind and body;
- over-focuses mind's attention;

- contracts mind and body, which is a form of exclusion;
- cuts off and suppresses the hindrances;
- creates resistance while supporting the false belief of a personal self (attā);
- without awareness of how craving arises.

In contrast, **a properly developed mind** using Tranquil Wisdom Insight Meditation:

- operates without tension or tightness,
- opens up mind's attention and sharpens awareness;
- expands mind's attention;
- allows the hindrances without conflict;
- opens up to a wider impersonal observation (anattā);
- sees and understands HOW craving arises.

In this way, all ideas of I/Me/Mine and such concepts (attā) are relinquished and the true nature of all existence is naturally seen through the eyes of Dhamma.

- A true meditative mind can be very still and composed without exercising suppression, exclusion, or resistance in it.
- A true meditative mind sees HOW mind's attention moves from the breath and relaxing, or mettā and relaxing, to being on an arising distraction and thinking.
- A true meditative mind, by practicing the 6R's, emphasizes Right Effort,
- sees HOW the hindrances are important to recognize
- and through the repetition of their arising, they begin to teach the meditator how craving works.
- A true meditative mind sees HOW this impersonal process of Dependent Origination actually occurs.

This is HOW "purity of mind" and "proper investigation" are developed.

The habit of investigating one's experience is a very important aspect of our spiritual growth.

When one is caught by a pain, distraction, or any hindrance, they must be able to see how mind reacts to that particular situation.

Overcoming Sloth and Torpor

Sloth and Torpor occur when the meditator experiences sleepiness and dullness arising while meditating.

The way to overcome sleepiness is by becoming more attentive, with a joyful interest on the object of meditation.

One must try to see directly HOW their mind slips back to the sleepiness.

Question: Exactly HOW does mind's attention lose its attentiveness to the object of meditation? What happens first?

Answer: Mind begins to lightly think this or that, without going back to the breath and relaxing.

Question: What happens next?

Answer: Mind then becomes kind of dreamy.

Question: What happens next?

Answer: The meditator's sitting posture begins to slump.

Question: What happens next?

Answer: Now the meditators head begins to bob up and down and the sloth and torpor have really set in.

At this time, the meditator must put sincerer interest into their object of meditation and be able to watch this process occur.

With sincerer interest in this way, the meditator will pick up their effort and energy into the practice.

When the meditator notices HOW mind's attention first starts to be caught by the hindrance, and they 6R it, they will let go of it more quickly and not be caught for too long a time.

If the meditator straightens up their back so it is almost over-straight, not enough to bring up pain, but almost, then, when the meditator notices that their back is starting to slump, they see this and straighten up their posture.

At that time the meditator has improved their mindfulness and they won't get caught quite as much.

With the improved mindfulness the meditator can then begin to see the other things when they arise and the sloth and torpor will fade away by themselves.

Another thing that can be very helpful is for the meditator to get up, if they have sat for at least 30 minutes, and do their walking meditation.

The meditator should pick a spot, on even ground, where they can walk in a straight line that is 30 to 40 feet long.

The meditator then walks to the end of their walking space and stops.

Now, without turning around, the meditator begins to walk backwards—all the while staying on the object of meditation.

When they reach the end of their walking space, they then walk forward to the end and stop to walk backwards again.

Do this for at least 20 minutes and walk at a normal to fast pace.

The purpose of this is to pick up energy and walk at a normal to fast pace to give the body some much needed exercise, so that the blood will flow more easily again.

The meditator then goes back to their sitting meditation while they stay with the breath and relaxing, or with their mettā and relaxing, and then their sitting will not have sloth arising.

Please remember: Mind's attention may 'ping pong' back and forth from the meditation object back to the sleepiness.

The lighter (meaning actual sunlight or bright light) and joyful interest and curiosity about how mind works, the more quickly the meditator will let go of the hindrance of sloth and torpor.

Understanding and Managing Pain

Similarly, when pain arises, one does not direct mind's attention into the pain.

The meditator can see how mind has resistance (aversion) to that sensation only when mind's attention is pulled to the pain.

If the meditator starts to think about or get involved with the pain, it will cause the pain to get bigger and more intense.

Please remember, every time the meditator tries to control or force the pain away with their thoughts, or to make the pain be the way they want it to be, actually, the meditator is identifying personally with that sensation and their personal dislike of the situation then makes the sensation get bigger and more intense;

The meditator is trying to control their feeling with their thoughts, and again, this makes the feeling greater than before.

The meditator now shifts into a mode of action towards the solution for this situation by beginning to practice the cycle of the 6R's.

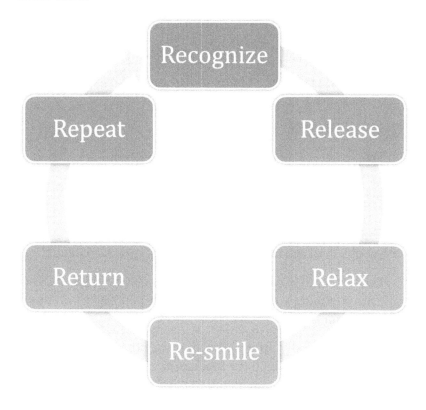

1) **The first "R" is the Recognize step.**

This is when the meditator realizes the change in tension and tightness in their mind and body as the sensation arises and becomes more intense;

2) **The second "R" is the Release step**.

The meditator lets go of the thinking mind, which verbalizes these distractions (pain, hindrance, heavy emotion, etc.);

3) **The third "R" is the Relax step.**

The meditator relaxes mind and releases the tight mental knot around the sensation, and relaxes the tightness in the head, so that mind naturally becomes calm;

4) **The fourth "R" is the Re-smile step.**

This is where the meditator smiles and brings up a wholesome object;

5) **The fifth "R" is the Return step.**

This means the meditator redirects mind's attention back to the object of meditation;

6) **The sixth "R" is the Repeat step**.

The meditator repeats this cycle as needed by staying on the object of meditation until another distraction occurs.

This is the 6R's meditation cycle in action and this is to be done continually until the pain doesn't pull mind's attention to it again.

This is decidedly different from some other meditation instructions, in which the meditators put their attention into the middle of the pain and note it as "pain. . . pain. . . pain.".

This kind of attention on the pain does cause the pain to get much bigger and last longer!

But pain by nature is repulsive and thus the meditators who practice this kind of noting have the tendency to tighten and harden mind's attention each time it is placed on the pain.

This causes tension to arise habitually in both mind and head (body).

In that way, although they can continue watching the pain, there evolves a hardening of mind through the false belief of a personal self,

in this case craving and clinging to **"my pain"** is never understood by the meditator nor is it ever seen clearly HOW the pain arises.

This hardening of mind's attention is actually "craving" and the thoughts about it are called "clinging."

Although these meditators may eventually, one day, develop enough equanimity to be able to overcome the distraction caused by the pain during meditation, it will take a very long time and there will be much suffering.

In other words, this one-pointed approach of concentration leads away from the true realization of How "craving" arises and How the meditator can allow it to cease.

The meditator will eventually clearly understand the purpose of the spiritual base of investigation (**dhammavicaya**):

The investigation is to purify mind by allowing everything that happens in the present moment to be there without trying to fight with, control, or disturb it in any way.

Loving-acceptance and patience (which is defined in the English dictionary as meaning non-aversion) of the present moment is the way to attain Nibbāna.

This is what the Buddha has said on many occasions!

The Five Faculties

Again, Udāyin, I have proclaimed to my disciples the way to develop the five spiritual faculties.

Here a person develops the faculty of faith (saddha) which leads to peace, leads to awakening.

The faculty of **faith** is also called the faculty of **"confidence."**

As a meditator becomes interested in letting go of the pain of living, their curiosity becomes stronger.

Thus, they begin to look for a meditation teacher.

If the meditator is fortunate enough to learn from a competent teacher who includes the teaching of how Dependent Origination actually occurs,

they will begin to see some slight changes in the way they perceive the world.

As the meditator begins to see and understand this through direct practice, their confidence will grow and then the meditator will use this patience in their daily life!

As a result, the meditator's enthusiasm towards the practice becomes more persistent and they will want to practice more often!

He develops the faculty of energy (vīriya), which leads to peace, leads to awakening.

When one's confidence grows, they will naturally put more **energy** into their practice.

The meditator begins to sit a little longer and mind becomes a little clearer.

The meditator needs to realize that during the meditation it is necessary to adjust the amount of energy they put into observing.

- If mind becomes dreamy or dull, then it is best to increase the level of attention and interest in observing.
- If mind becomes restless then the meditator may find it necessary to relax the amount of energy they are putting into observing.

When restlessness arises, the meditator should make sure *not to move the body at all*, for any reason.

Of course, this is the first thing you want to do! Be still.

It is best to sit without moving and bring up a sincere feeling of peace and tranquility.

This will help mind to settle down again.

How Long Should the Meditator Sit?

For the beginner it is recommended to sit not less than 30 minutes at a time.

When a sitting is good, please stay with that sitting for as long as it lasts.

A good sitting is when mind's attention is able to stay on the meditation object for a period of time.

It is good to sit for progressively longer periods of time and not worry about becoming attached to the sitting.

The only way one becomes attached is by thinking about and not using the 6R's in the correct manner.

There is nothing wrong in sitting for long periods of time as long as the meditator does not hurt themselves physically and they have enough exercise.

Sitting for one or two or three hours is fine only when one is ready to sit comfortably for such long hours.

It is never good to push oneself or use force in order to sit for long periods of time.

The meditator must remember that this is a natural process and trying to sit for too long can cause physical problems when one is pushing too hard.

If one sits in a particular way that causes pain to arise every time, then they are causing themselves unnecessary physical discomfort.

Please don't sit in that position again.

Please adjust your body position.

What is Meditation Pain?

There are two different kinds of pain that a meditator can experience while doing the meditation.

There is "real pain" and there is "meditation pain."

The way to tell the difference is this:

REAL PAIN

When the meditator is doing their sitting meditation and a pain arises, sometimes the pain can be quite intense.

When the meditator gets up from their sitting practice, if the pain stays or becomes worse, then please don't sit in that way again.

This is a "real pain" and it can cause some real physical problems for the meditator, if they continue to sit that way again.

The meditation is not about causing permanent damage to the body.

It is not about biting the bullet and making oneself suffer!

It is about seeing the true nature of HOW Dependent Origination actually occurs.

Meditators don't have to torture themselves or cause physical damage to themselves; this is unskillful practice.

Finding a posture that has very little pain arising in it is best!

Sometimes if the meditator sits in a chair, it can bring relief.

If the meditator is already sitting in a chair and the real pain comes up, then find a different chair that is more comfortable or do the standing meditation.

If this is comfortable then continue using this posture.

One thing that happens for a lot of meditators is: they sit until a pain arises then they shift their sitting posture and sit for a longer period of time.

Please don't do that!

The walking meditation is an important part of the meditation; it is not a disturbance or break in the meditation!

Instead of changing the posture so that the meditator can stay sitting, it is by far better for the meditator to get up and do the walking meditation.

The meditator needs to move and get their blood circulating again.

The walking meditation can be better than the sitting meditation sometimes and when it is then continue walking for up to 45 minutes.

Then come back while still staying on your meditation object and smiling, then sit again in a comfortable posture.

Meditation Pain

The other kind of pain that can sometimes arise can be just as intense as the real pain, but when the meditator gets up to do the walking meditation the pain goes away after a short period of time.

This is called a "meditation pain."

When the meditator recognizes this kind of pain, it is best to sit through it without moving at all.

The author promises that if the meditator does this, they will have some wonderful experiences when the pain fades away by itself. Promise!

Having a Blank Mind Experience

One comical thing that occasionally happens when a meditator does very little walking is that they come to the teacher with this wonderful experience of having mind completely go blank.

It is just as if someone were to wipe a chalk-board clean!

The meditator then thinks they have had some mystical/magical, spiritual experience.

After questioning the meditator, the teacher finds out that they have not done any walking meditation all day

Then, the teacher has to tell the meditator that this is absolutely nothing!

It is just a form of sloth and torpor and they have to do the walking meditation for a while.

In this way, the student can pick up their energy and not get caught by the sloth again.

What is the Proper Sitting Position?

There is no secret sitting method that leads straight to awakening.

There is no secret in any floor or cushion!

Some meditators are as flexible as rubber and can sit in any position but this is not mandatory for success in the meditation.

People in Asia grow up sitting a lot on the floor and are comfortable doing this.

The position of half lotus or full lotus is common amongst them.

People in the West did not grow up sitting on the floor!

For the most part, they grew up sitting on chairs and sofas and benches.

To understand about how we should sit, we should first become aware of what the Buddha was actually doing.

He was performing a Mind yoga in order to see clearly how everything works!

This was not a body yoga.

This exercise of investigating the mind can be done in a sitting, standing, walking, or lying down posture.

It was not meant to be a physically painful experience.

Using the lying down position before you really understand what you are doing is not advised, because most likely you will fall asleep.

Sitting, walking, and standing are the best positions for learning the meditation and perfecting your understanding.

Sit in a way that you are comfortable and be sure your legs are supported properly, especially your knees.

If you are on the floor, you may wish to form a nest to sit in, so your knees will not become stressed.

The good news for modern man here is that it is all right if the meditator uses a stool or chair, as long as the chair is not too soft, offers proper support, and they do not lean heavily back into the chair.

There is a line of energy, which flows up the back, and this should not be cut off.

Leaning is good for sleeping and dullness, not meditating!

In order to avoid sagging or slouching, the meditator should sit nicely straight but not stiffly erect.

The spine should be comfortably straight.

Place a rolled towel or small pillow at the base of the spine to keep it slightly away from the back of the chair.

Some people prefer a sitting bench.

Many kinds of low and higher benches have been designed.

The point here is to be able to sit comfortably straight and alert, so that you can observe carefully what is going on.

When in a comfortable and correct sitting posture, the more confidence the meditator has and the more energy they will put into their practice.

The meditator's enthusiasm will naturally increase too.

Developing the Faculty of Mindfulness

He develops the faculty of mindfulness (sati) which leads to peace, leads to awakening.

Taken from the Satipaṭṭhāna Sutta # 10 section #8 in the Majjhima Nikāya: this section gives an explanation of mindfulness and is called "Full Awareness." It says:

A person is one who acts with full awareness when going forward and returning;

Who acts with full awareness when looking ahead and looking away;

Who acts with full awareness when flexing and extending his limbs;

Who acts with full awareness when wearing his robes and carrying his outer robe and bowl;

Who acts with full awareness when eating, drinking, consuming food and tasting;

Who acts with full awareness when defecating and urinating;

Who acts with full awareness when walking, standing, sitting, falling asleep, waking up, talking, and keep silent.

The real question here is "full awareness" of what?

The answer that most teachers and students will tell you is that this means to be aware of the body, but that answer is wrong!

The answer actually is to "keep a full awareness of what mind's attention is doing," while the person makes all of these bodily movements.

In the first verse of the Dhammapada it says:

Mind is the forerunner of all unwholesome states, mind made are they, when one speaks or acts with an unwholesome mind, pain will follow as surely as the hoof of the draft ox.

The second verse says:

Mind is the forerunner of all wholesome states, mind-made are they, when one speaks or acts with a wholesome mind, happiness will follow even as one's shadow that never leaves.

As one's energy improves, their awareness and mindfulness will naturally become stronger.

This meditation is a very natural "un-forced" observation process leading to understanding.

Let's take a look at an ordinary person's mind, a person like you or me.

As we first begin meditating what we find is a "grasshopper mind," a "butterfly mind," or one could also say a "mad monkey mind."

It is ever-moving, ever-jumping around.

It changes its concepts, fantasies, and impulses all of the time.

Mind is a prey for arising stimuli, which are its own personal attachments, and emotional reactions.

This jumping around of mind and taking personally whatever arises is a re-action to the stimuli.

The meditator is mostly **re-acting** to impulses the way they always act when a certain kind of stimuli arises.

It is a chain of linked associations, hopes, fears, memories, fantasies, regrets, streaming constantly through mind, triggered by memories of the outside world.

Mind is blindly never-stopping, and never-satisfied in its search for pleasure and satisfaction.

It is no wonder that mind becomes so crazy and filled with un-satisfactoriness and was described as a restless "mad monkey" swinging from branch-to-branch in the quest for a satisfying piece of fruit through the endless jungle of conditional events.

Thus, when one first begins to meditate, mind naturally runs all over the place and stays away from the "object of meditation" for a long time.

Sometimes it even takes two or three minutes before one is able to recognize this movement, they then gently let it go, relax the tension in the head, calm mind, re-smile, and re-direct the attention back to the breath and relaxing. (The 6R's).

This condition of mind running around is only natural, because monkey-mind is used to running wherever it likes and thinking whatever it likes.

But as the meditator's practice develops and they are able to 6R mind's attention wandering around, recognize, and let go more quickly, their mindfulness gradually becomes sharper.

Mind's attention might only stay away from the breath or mettā for one minute, before 6Ring, and recognizing that it is not on the breath or mettā.

The meditator then let's go, relaxes mind, smiles, and comes back to the breath and relaxing or mettā and relaxing.

This is called gradual training.

At this time mind begins to stay on the breath or mettā for longer periods of time.

Perhaps it stays as long as thirty seconds before it goes off again.

Of course, when a beginner starts the meditation the 6R's are pretty new and it takes a little while to get used to using them. This is only natural!

As the meditator begins to let go of verbalizing the 6R's, and they get into a flowing motion with the 6R's, then mind begins to become more alert and observant.

Then the meditator's mindfulness or observation power becomes stronger and the meditation becomes easier.

However, the meditator is now becoming better at seeing when mind's attention goes away and HOW it moves from one thing to another.

The meditator's mindfulness becomes sharper and they are able to recognize what mind's attention is doing!

They begin to observe a repeating process.

Thus, when the meditator's confidence improves even better, their energy improves and as a result the alertness of mind naturally develops.

That is how the faculty of **mindfulness** is developed.

He develops the faculty of collectedness (samādhi), which leads to peace, leads to awakening.

When one's 6R's and mindfulness of the present moment improves, mind's attention will naturally stay on the object of meditation for much longer periods of time.

Most people would describe this as concentration, but this is not as accurate or precise a description as it could be.

Mind's attention is not absorbed into, fixed on, or glued to the object of meditation.

This is because there is no information in that object of meditation.

Instead, mind's attention is very still, relaxed, collected, and composed, naturally staying on the breath or mettā very well with almost no effort at all.

At this time a strong feeling of "joy" arises and the body becomes very light and feels as if it is floating.

The meditator realizes that this is a pleasant feeling and 6R's it, too!

Pleasant feeling and painful feeling are two sides of the same coin and both kinds of feeling are treated in exactly the same way, that is, they are 6Red.

Eventually, when the "joy" fades away, a powerful feeling of tranquility, equanimity, and comfortableness (happiness) arises.

Due to the meditator's keen mindfulness and full awareness, they do not become involved with these feelings.

If the meditator begins to think or internally verbalize about how nice this state is, and how much they like it, they will lose that state and sleepiness very often comes into mind.

This is because the meditator is caught by the attachment to those feelings (craving or the "I like it" mind—attā) and attention slips off without coming back to the breath and smiling, or mettā and smiling.

Mindfulness fades away when one starts to think or internally verbalize about things and mind becomes involved in wanting to personally control these thoughts and feelings.

This also happens when one desires the "joy," "tranquility," and happiness to arise.

This desire makes mind's attention try too hard and as a result restlessness and dissatisfaction arise, followed by lots of suffering!

Trying too hard makes mind's attention lean out of the present moment and then restlessness and suffering arises.

Something that seems to happen fairly often is that a meditator has a really good sitting and then they get up and do something.

When the meditator comes back to do another sitting meditation, they want to continue with some really good meditation again, but this desire makes them try a little too hard and their mind becomes restless.

The meditator thinks "I want" this to be a good sitting like before!

Now, they put even more energy into their meditation to make mind's attention settle down, but restlessness becomes even stronger!

The meditator starts to become frustrated and really tries to make mind's attention stay on the object of meditation.

Of course, mind's attention won't do that because of excessive energy and craving.

The meditator then runs to the teacher and begins to complain about how hard it is to be tranquil.

The teacher laughs and asks if there is "someone" who "wants" their meditation to be good?

Of course, the answer comes back "Yes, *I* do."

Then, generally, the meditator says something like, "Oh, *I* got caught again, didn't *I*?

The teacher then asks the student if they want to have a calm tranquil mind?

If so, then they have to stop trying so hard!

Again, the teacher asks if the student knows what is going to happen in the next five minutes?

The student says "No."

Then the teacher says, "Then why are you trying to make something happen in a particular way, if you don't know what will happen in the future?

Why are you pushing to have everything happen in the way you want it to be?"

In this case, as a meditator, you are leaning out of the present moment towards the next present moment because you want something to happen in a particular way!

Stop causing yourself so much pain and suffering, OK?

Relax! Have fun!

Laugh at how you have caused yourself so much pain by getting caught in the craving–clinging–habitual tendency cycle!

This kind of conceptual thinking causes mind to lose any sense of mindfulness or full awareness.

Thus, any balance and equanimity is completely gone.

Of course, this makes mind even more restless and the meditator suffers even more.

At that time mind becomes serious and the meditator really suffers and they think that this meditation doesn't work so well!

The fact is this meditation works very well, when the meditator follows the instructions closely and has a light, smiling mind!!!

These combinations of hindrances will stop all spiritual practice from occurring, because the 'wanting for things to be in a particular way' makes all the spiritual development fade away.

Therefore, one must be more mindful of the thoughts about these levels of pleasant abiding (jhāna).

Thus, as the use of the 6R's improves the meditator's confidence increases and energy grows.

This improves mindfulness, which enables mind's attention to be very collected and eventually mindfulness becomes stronger and lasts longer.

A monk develops the faculty of wisdom (or understanding of Dependent Origination) which leads to peace, leads to awakening.

And thereby many disciples of mine abide having reached the consummation and perfection of direct knowledge.

As the meditator's mind becomes more calm and still, they are able to see the true nature of things.

This development of **wisdom** or intelligence is gained by seeing HOW things arise and pass away (anicca) by themselves.

Even while one is sitting in a jhāna [a meditation stage] they see how, for instance, joy arises.

It is there for a while; then it fades away.

They see how tranquility and happiness arise.

They are there for a while and then they fade away.

The meditator is able to see the true nature of impermanence, even in the beginning of their practice, by observing thoughts arising and passing away.

The meditator observes feeling and emotions arising and passing away.

They also notice that these things that arise and pass away (anicca) are unsatisfactory (dukkha) and these feelings and emotions are a form of suffering, especially when they don't behave in the way we want them to.

When the meditator sees how truly unsatisfactory this process is, they clearly see that it is an impersonal process (anattā).

There is no one controlling the appearance and disappearance of these things.

Even while in jhāna [a meditation stage of understanding] the meditator has no real control over the joy arising, because joy arises when the conditions are right for it to come up.

At the same time, the meditator simply cannot force joy to stay, because it will fade away when the conditions are right.

This causes more un-satisfactoriness to arise, because joy is such a nice feeling!

Thus, one is able to see the characteristics of existence very clearly, i.e. anicca (impermanence), dukkha (suffering), and not-self (anattā).

This is the way to develop **wisdom**, which gradually leads the meditator to the seeing of all of the links of Dependent Origination both arising and passing away (that is, seeing and fully realizing The Four Noble Truths).

An interesting observation is that one can see the three characteristics of existence without ever seeing Dependent Origination, but they can never see Dependent Origination without seeing the three characteristics of existence (i.e., impermanence, suffering and not-self/impersonal nature) at the same time.

This can be discussed in more depth and detail at a later time.

The Five Powers

Again Udāyin, I have proclaimed to my disciples the way to develop the Five Spiritual Powers.

Here a person develops the Power of Faith, which leads to peace, leads to awakening.

They develop the Power of Energy, which leads to peace, leads to awakening.

They develop the Power of Mindfulness, which leads to peace, leads to awakening.

They develop the Power of Collectedness, which leads to peace, leads to awakening.

They develop the Power of Wisdom, which leads to peace, leads to awakening.

And thereby many disciples of mine abide having reached the consummation and perfection of direct knowledge.

These are the same as the five faculties mentioned above.

They are called powers because of their ability to purify mind and make it wholesome and clean.

The faculties become powers when they are seen and used automatically at the correct time.

It is the practice of Right Effort that makes this development occur automatically.

We will now continue with the Ānāpānasati Sutta.

14] In this Saṅgha of monks there are monks who abide devoted to the development of loving-kindness - such monks are there in this Saṅgha of Monks.

In this Saṅgha of monks there are monks who abide devoted to the development of compassion - such monks are there in this Saṅgha of Monks.

In this Saṅgha of monks there are monks who abide devoted to the development of appreciative joy - such monks are there in this Saṅgha of Monks

In this Saṅgha of monks there are monks who abide devoted to the development of equanimity - such monks are there in this Saṅgha of Monks.

In this Saṅgha of monks there are monks who abide devoted to the development of the meditation of foulness - such monks are there in this Saṅgha of Monks.

In this Saṅgha of monks there are monks who abide devoted to the development of the perception of impersonality - such monks are there in this Saṅgha of Monks.

In this Saṅgha of Monks there are monks who abide devoted to the development of Mindfulness of Breathing - such monks are there in this Saṅgha of Monks.

Loving-kindness, compassion, selfless joy and equanimity are known as the Four "Brahma Vihāras" or the Four Boundless states of mind, or the Limitless states of mind.

This is because there is no boundary or limitations to one's mind, when they are in these meditative states.

The meditation of foulness is suitable for those who have a strong affinity for lust arising in their minds.

It is practiced by reflecting on the individual elements of the body and the disgusting nature of one's body parts.

For example, when one looks at a beautiful person and thoughts of lust arise, they can imagine how desirable that person would be if all of their body parts where to be turned inside-out!

Will one's mind think,

> "Oh! what a lovely intestine or liver!" or
> "Wow! What beautiful bile, pus, and phlegm that person has!"

How much lust is there in mind at that time?

Thus, this meditation helps people with a lustful personality to become more balanced.

The perception of impermanence does not actually refer to sitting down and thinking about how everything changes.

It is about seeing how rapidly the links of Dependent Origination arise and pass away.

This is about realizing that this process happens so quickly that there cannot be any chance for a personal self (attā) that directs it.

Remember: Tranquil Wisdom Insight Meditation is about seeing with a silent and spacious mind.

Deeply seeing and understanding how Dependent Origination works refers to the meditation states of infinite space and infinite consciousness where mind sees just how fleeting these mental and physical phenomena truly are.

We will now proceed to the next section of the sutta, which speaks about Mindfulness of Breathing.

Mindfulness of Breathing

15] Monks, when mindfulness of breathing is developed and cultivated, it is of great fruit and great benefit.

When Mindfulness of Breathing is developed and cultivated, it fulfills the Four Foundations of Mindfulness.

When the Four Foundations of Mindfulness are developed and cultivated, they fulfill the Seven Enlightenment Factors.

When the Seven Enlightenment Factors are developed and cultivated, they fulfill true knowledge and deliverance.

One observes that the Four Foundations of Mindfulness are in this sutta and they are fulfilled through the practice of jhāna or tranquil and wise (samatha/vipassanā) meditative states of mind.

This is decidedly different from the current theory that one can't fulfill the Four Foundations of Mindfulness, while experiencing jhāna [meditative stages of understanding].

The Buddha only taught one kind of meditation and that is samatha or serenity or one can say he taught Samadhi— Tranquil Wisdom

Insight Meditation' (samatha/vipassanā).

16] And how, monks, is mindfulness of breathing developed and cultivated, so that it is of great fruit and great benefit?

17] Here a monk, gone to the forest or to the root of a tree or an empty hut, sits down;

having folded his legs crosswise, set his body erect, and established mindfulness in front of him,

ever mindful he breathes in (and relaxes), mindful he breathes out (and relaxes).

The phrase "gone to the forest or to the root of a tree or an empty hut" means that one goes to a reasonably quiet place where there will be few distractions.

A suitable location would be one that is away from road noises, loud and persistent music or sounds, people as well as animals.

During the time of the Buddha most people sat on floors.

Hence, the phrase "sits down; having folded his legs crosswise, set his body erect."

But today, sitting on the floor can be a very trying and painful experience as people in the west mostly sit on chairs, stools, or couches.

If one wants to sit on floors, it may help if they sit on cushions.

In actual fact, it is far more important to observe what is happening with mind's attention than to sit with uncomfortable or painful sensations.

Remember: **there is no magic in sitting on the floor.**

The magic comes from a clear, calm mind that is at ease, open and craving-free as much of the time as possible.

Thus, if sitting on the floor is a very painful experience, then simply sit on a stool or a chair, without making a big deal out of it.

There is however, an extremely important factor if the meditator sits on a chair.

"Set his body erect" means sit with a nicely straight back, which is not rigid and uncomfortable.

A nicely straight back has all of the vertebrae stacked one upon another.

This is to ensure that energy can flow up and down the back without any blockages.

Leaning stops the energy flow and causes sleepiness to arise.

When the meditator first starts out, their back is not used to being straight and some of the muscles can rebel and complain.

However, with patience and perseverance, these unused muscles will gradually adjust and strengthen.

There is another important aspect to sitting meditation.

One must *sit without moving the body for any reason.*

The meditator can move around as much as a Buddha image, which means to say, not at all!

Please do not wriggle the toes or fingers or move the hands to rub or scratch or change the posture in any way or rock back and forth until after the sitting is over.

Any movement breaks the continuity of the practice and this causes the meditator to start all over again.

Some meditation teachers tell their students that it is quite all right to move as long as they are "mindful."

But if the students are truly mindful, they would be able to watch mind's attention and its dislike of the sensations and then relax mind of its aversion.

Thus, there is **no reason to move**!

Mindfulness means to lovingly-observe what is happening in the present moment, without trying to control, resist, or change it.

To be truly mindful means to open up and allow whatever presents itself in the present moment.

Moving while sitting means that the meditator is not being mindful at all.

If the meditator is giving in to the desire to move, they are identifying with that desire (attā).

Thus, when one is ready and begins to meditate, they must remain still and keep letting go and tranquilizing mind whenever there is a distraction.

Actually the only allowable movement during meditation is to straighten the back when it starts to curve or slump, as long as it is not done too often.

The phrase **"establishing mindfulness in front of him"** means that one puts aside all other worldly affairs and involvement with sensual pleasures.

The meditator softly closes the eyes and whenever there is a distracting sound, smell, taste, sensation, or thought, they are aware of it and simply let it go.

Then the meditator relaxes any remaining tightness in the head and redirects the smiling attention back to the object of meditation.

The Walking Meditation

(This section is a repeat from "How" beginning on page 136)

One thing to observe before we go to the walking meditation is:

The walking meditation is a very important part of the training and needs to be practiced!!!

Please do *NOT* change your posture because the body wants to be **relieved** from some discomfort, and then continue doing the sitting meditation.

The meditator is learning a few things from this part of the practice and it has to do with learning to be mindful in one's daily life, as well as getting exercise for the body.

When you are ready, after sitting for no less than 30 minutes, then please do the walking meditation.

The meditator stays with their object of meditation i.e. the breath and relaxing, or the mettā and relaxing. Do not change to focusing on the body movements. Stay on your home object.

Please don't place mind's attention on the feet while walking, or begin walking very slowly, like other teachers advise.

If the meditator walks with their mind's attention on their feet, then they are not very aware of what mind's attention is doing.

Why? Because the meditator is not watching what mind's attention is doing and they are trying to over-focus on just the movements of the feet.

The question that needs to be asked here is, "Is the meditator being truly mindful of HOW mind's attention moves from one thing to another, when they are over-focusing on only the movement of the feet?"

The meditator needs to walk at a regular pace just like they do when walking from one place to another, in their normal life!

There are some real advantages to walking this way because the blood starts moving around better and one's body gets some exercise so muscles can stretch out and let any stiffness go.

Walking in a normal to fast pace also energizes one's body so sloth or torpor won't become as much of a problem.

When the meditator is doing walking meditation they need to keep their eyes down, not be looking around.

Why? Because where the eyes go, so goes mind's attention.

Before too long, mind is thinking this or that and is completely distracted and not aware of the object of meditation

The meditator stays on the breath and relaxing, or, mettā and relaxing, using the 6R's whenever mind's attention gets distracted.

At first, mind's attention will be somewhat active and lots of wandering thoughts will invade it.

But, with calm patience in 6Ring, those distractions will eventually settle down and the meditator will be able to stay with their object of meditation.

Eventually, the walking meditation will become as good as the sitting meditation.

This way, when one is off of retreat they can bring their meditation into their daily activities more easily.

It is recommended that the student walk fast enough so the heart beats a little more quickly and that they continue for at least 15 minutes.

When the meditation is good, they can walk for longer but not more than 45 minutes.

> *Ever mindful he breathes in (relaxes), mindful he breathes out (relaxes).*

This tells us the way to practice mindfulness of breathing.

An important thing to realize is that: *the breath is the reminder for the meditator to relax all tensions and tightnesses in both one's body and mind!*

Being aware of the breath means to know when one is experiencing the in-breath and relaxing and to know when one is experiencing the out-breath and relaxing.

It simply means to open up one's awareness and to be attentive to the breath and relaxing as much as possible and at the same time, relax the tightness in the head (this will be explained more thoroughly in a little while).

Meditation Instructions

> *18] Breathing in long, he understands: 'I breathe in long'; or breathing out long, he understands: 'I breathe out long.'*
>
> *Breathing in short, he understands: 'I breathe in short'; or breathing out short he understands 'I breathe out short.'*

The words **"he understands"** are emphasized here to show that one does not focus with strong attention on the breath to the exclusion of everything else.

One merely **understands** what the breath is doing in the present moment. That's all there is to this!

As to location of where the meditator puts their mind's attention.

Has anyone read any words like nostril, nostril tip, upper lip, lungs, or abdomen?

No? Why? Because they are not mentioned in these instructions!

The location of the meditators attention is not nearly so important as what they are doing when following the instructions given by the Buddha.

One simply knows when they breathe in long or short!

Please do this without attempting to control the breath at any time.

Instead, there is only understanding of what one is doing in the present moment.

If the meditator tries to "over-focus" or "concentrate" on the breath to the exclusion of anything else, they will develop a headache due to this "wrong concentration".

It is necessary to understand that the "breath" is not the only thing the meditator observes!

This full meditation is using the breath as a reminder to relax!

The meditator doesn't only focus on the breath, but they use the breath to help in relaxing the body and mind!

Whenever a meditator holds tightly onto the meditation object and tries to force mind to "concentrate" or bumps any distractions away, the head will develop a very tight and painful tension.

This tightness or tension on the head also occurs when the meditator attempts to control the sitting, by throwing down any distracting thoughts and feelings, and quickly rushing back to the meditation object.

This happens with "momentary concentration" as well as any other kind of one-pointed concentration technique.

Many meditation teachers tell their students to put their attention right in the middle of the sensation and see its true nature.

This will cause a few different things to occur.

First, the students will develop a stronger pain and this becomes a true distraction instead.

It is because these meditation teachers tell their students to stay with that pain until it goes away.

Unfortunately, this can take an unbelievably long time.

Secondly, the students need to tighten and toughen mind in order to observe the tension.

Actually, this tightening and toughening of mind is not being fully mindful.

The students begin to develop a mind that hardens itself when pain arises.

It is only natural that this happens, since it takes a lot of courage and fortitude to watch pain in this way.

A type of aversion is naturally developed at that time, and this hardening of mind is not being noticed as anicca, dukkha, and anattā.

Consequently, even when one is not "meditating," this suppression can cause personality hardening, and that causes true problems to arise.

Mind has a tendency to become critical and judgmental and the personality development of the meditator becomes hard and unmindful in their daily activities.

Many people say they need to do a loving-kindness retreat after doing other types of meditation, because they discovered that they do and say things, which are not so nice to other people.

When this happens, a question arises.

"Is this really a type of meditation technique which leads to my happiness and to the happiness of others?"

"If the answer is yes, then why do I need to practice another form of meditation to balance my thinking?"

Eventually one is able to suppress this aversion by practicing "concentration," which is taught to be the "correct method" by most meditation teachers.

The method taught by the Buddha was to *never suppress anything.*

His method was to open, expand, and discover HOW mind's attention moves and to allow everything that arises in the present moment.

This is true mindfulness.

Thus, whenever any kind of pain arises (emotional or physical) in mind or body,

- one first recognizes that mind's attention has gone to that sensation,
- then the meditator 6R's it by letting go of any thoughts about that sensation and relaxes,
- then opens mind and let's go of the tight mental fist that is wrapped around the sensation, or by letting

the sensation be there by itself without any mental resistance or aversion to it.

This is done by telling themselves, "Never mind it is all right for this pain to be there."

- Next, relax the tightness, which is in the head—feel mind expand and become calm
- then re-smile and
- redirect mind's attention back to the object of meditation, i.e. the breath and relaxing.

If one gets caught in the thinking about the sensation or pain, the sensation will get bigger and become more intense.

One thing to recognize is that we human beings are made up of five different things called aggregates. They are: the physical body, feeling, perception, formations (where thoughts are predominant), and consciousness.

Our habit is that whenever a painful feeling arises we try to think our feeling away.

This makes the painful feeling much bigger and more intense.

Eventually, the meditator can't stand it anymore and feel that they have to move.

This thinking or internally verbalizing about the sensation and wishing it would go away is the "ego identification" taking the painful sensation personally (attā).

This getting involved with, trying to control, fighting with the sensation, resisting the sensation, or trying to make the feeling be the way we want it to be is only fighting with the Dhamma (Truth of the Present Moment).

Whenever anyone fights and tries to control or hardens mind to the Dhamma of the present moment, they cause themselves undue suffering and pain.

Another way of fighting with Dhamma is by taking the sensation personally,

then trying to control it because it is "Mine" (attā).

This worsens the pain and as a result, it hurts even more.

This is true DUKKHA – suffering!

Thus, one must learn to openly and lovingly accept the present moment without that "ego-identification" and the thinking, internally verbalization about, or taking it as "I am that."

This is how one gains calmness and composure of mind, as well as equanimity, full awareness, and mindfulness.

The Buddha taught us three kinds of actions while meditating or during our daily activities.

They are:
1. **Love Where We Are;**
2. **Love What We Are Doing in the Present Moment;**
3. **Love Who We Are With.**

These simple explanations allow one to be completely accepting of the present moment.

"To Love where We Are" means to accept the fact that when the meditator is sitting in meditation or when they are doing their daily activities in life, things are not always like we want them to be, so we need to soften mind's attention and allow whatever is there to be there without keeping mind's attention on it.

This is true loving-acceptance of the present moment.

"To Love What We Are Doing" means to open up mind and allow whatever arises in the present moment, to present itself without our getting attached to it.

A good acronym for this is **"DROPSS"** which means *"Don't Resist Or Push. Soften and Smile"*!

Whatever arises, one does not resist or push, ever.

Just learn to practice the 6R's, so that you can then soften into it, open mind, and accept it.

In other words, **"Love What We Are Doing."**

"To Love Who We Are With" means to love yourself enough so that you can see and let go of all kinds of attachments, which cause pain to arise in body and mind.

The recognition that a person causes their own suffering is a major realization.

The meditator cannot ever blame the world or other individuals for their own suffering.

This fact was actually one of the main reasons that the author became so interested in the Buddha's path.

Learning to take responsibility for our own situation and suffering is a big lesson to understand.

When one truly loves themselves, they will see the pain and sorrow and lovingly let it go by practicing the 6R's.

This is done by letting go of the "thinking about."

The thinking mind needs our attention on it in order to grow.

When the meditator re-directs their attention away from those thoughts, then they will simply lose energy and fade away by themselves.

Thus, they let go of the attachment by relaxing the craving and the ego identification (attā) with it.

> *He trains thus: 'I shall breathe in experiencing the whole body'; he trains thus 'I shall breathe out experiencing the whole body';*

This part of the instructions means that the meditator is fully aware of where there is tension or tightness in their body and mind.

The meditator doesn't have to over-focus mind or "concentrate" on the breath, or take this breathing as the object of extreme concentration'.

One simply *knows* what body and mind are doing in the present moment.

The meditator's mindfulness is sharp enough to know what the breath and their body are doing at all times,

without controlling the breath in any way.

Just let the breath be and relaxing awareness is a natural process.

> *He trains thus: 'I shall breathe in tranquilizing the bodily formation'; he trains thus: 'I shall breathe out tranquilizing the bodily formation.'*

This simple statement is the *most important part* of the meditation instructions.

It is also the most neglected part of the instructions for the Breathing Meditation!

Strange to tell!

It is a remarkable omission that is actually the key difference between the Buddha's meditation instructions and the absorption, one-pointed concentration!

This part of the instructions directs the meditator to notice the tension or tightness, which arises in the head with every arising of a consciousness, and to let that tightness go, while on the in-breath and out-breath.

Every person has a thin membrane wrapped around their brain; it is called the "meninges."

Whenever mind's attention moves from one thing to another, this causes that membrane to contract or get tight.

Sometimes this can be quite big and easy to see and sometimes it is very subtle and difficult to recognize.

The Buddha's instructions are very clear here!

He says to relax on the in-breath and to relax on the out-breath.

What this does is it makes the meditator more aware of the subtleties of HOW craving actually does arise!

Please remember that **craving always manifests as a tension or tightness in one's body and mind.**

The craving mind is the mind that automatically comes as the "I like it" or "I don't like it" mind arises.

When a pleasant feeling arises then the craving "I like it," "I want it," "I want this to last" mind arises.

This is seen by one's sincere attention as a tightness or tension in one's mind and brain (body).

When a painful feeling arises then mind automatically has the craving mind arise and it is the "I don't like it," "I don't want it," "I want this to stop and go away" mind.

This also is seen by one's sincere attention as a tightness or tension in one's mind and brain (body).

Being fully aware of this subtle tightness or tension while breathing in and breathing out is **very important**!

This extra step the Buddha added to the breathing meditation changes the entire process of meditation.

It also changes the end result of the meditation.

Why? Because, when the meditator practices the 6R's, they are letting go of craving and this purifies mind's attention.

What this means is that the meditator begins to see for themselves HOW the impersonal process of Dependent Origination actually does work.

This true understanding leads the meditator onward to the final end-result of the experience of Nibbāna!

When one feels mind open up, expand, relax, smile, and become tranquil, this is what the Buddha called the Third Noble Truth or the Cessation of Suffering.

He also called this "Wisdom's Eye," which is seeing clearly without any craving.

Every time the meditator sees that mind is distracted away from the breath and relaxing, they simply practice the 6R's and let go of the distraction and then relax any remaining tightness in the head by letting go one step further.

They feel mind become open, expanded, relaxed, calm and clear.

This is called relieving oneself of "craving"!

Next, one softly re-smiles and re-directs mind's attention back to the in-breath and relax; feel the expanded calm and relax tightness in the head and mind;

Then continue on the out-breath to relax, expanding the calm then relaxing the tension in the head and mind.

For example, when a thought arises, just let the thought go and 6R it.

Don't continue thinking, even if one is in mid-sentence.

Just softly practice the 6R's and let the thought go without getting caught in the content of the thoughts.

If the distraction is a sensation, first, open mind and let go of the aversion to the sensation, then 6R it, open and expand mind and smile before re-directing mind's attention back to the breath and relaxing.

This opening up, expanding and letting go of the tightness in the head is actually letting go of craving and the subtle 'ego identification' which attaches itself to everything as it arises.

Thus, when the meditator lets go of this tension, they are actually letting go of all craving, then mind's attention becomes clear, alert and has no distractions in it.

When the meditation instructions here are followed closely, there will be no "sign or nimitta" arising in mind (i.e., no lights or other kinds of mind-made objects, which arise in mind when one is practicing 'concentration meditation').

Mind naturally becomes calm, tranquil and very alert with true mindfulness and contentment.

The meditator doesn't need to try to force mind to stay on the object of meditation through strong concentration.

One begins to realize the true nature of all phenomena as being impermanent (anicca), unsatisfactory (dukkha), and not-self (anattā) and the meditator will see this through the impersonal (anattā) understanding of Dependent Origination.

Thus, those who practice Tranquil Wisdom Insight Meditation (TWIM), they are aware of the in-breath and at the same time, the relaxation of the tightness in the head and mind.

They are also aware of the out-breath and again at the same time the relaxation of the tightness in the head and mind.

It is no problem if the meditator happens to miss one in-breath or one out-breath at first.

They should not put unnecessary pressure on themselves which might cause them to think how difficult this practice is.

The practice of the 6R's makes this meditation easy to remember and to do. Plus, the 6R's can be done during the meditator's daily activities.

Therefore, the meditation easily translates into life!

This is actually an incredibly easy practice and a simple way to develop mind.

Thus, if one occasionally misses the in-breath or out-breath, just let it go and catch the next in-breath and relax or out-breath and relax.

Simple and easy, isn't it?

At first, the breath and relaxing may seem to be very fast and difficult to notice.

However, as one continues with their practice of the 6R's and smiling, the meditation becomes easier and they will not miss the in-breath or out-breath and relaxing that much.

After all, this is a gradual training.

There is no need to put undue pressure on oneself.

Simply relax and smile into the meditation.

Make this a fun game to play instead of a serious job to do!

When one practices Tranquil Wisdom Insight Meditation, the breath and relaxing do not become subtle and difficult to observe.

If the meditator has tightness arising in the head, then they are 'concentrating' too much and need to stop trying so hard!

If the meditator begins to get too serious about what they are doing, too much energy is being put into trying to accomplish something!

In this case, the tightness in the head is not relaxed enough and the 6R's are not being used enough.

If the breath seems to disappear again, the meditator is focusing on concentration and not tranquilizing mind enough.

The jhānas will appear by themselves as mind's attention becomes calm and peaceful.

The meditator does not have to push, force, or "concentrate with a fixed mind"!

Actually, the Buddha taught a most natural form of meditation that works for every type of personality or individual.

> *19] He trains thus: 'I shall breathe in experiencing joy';*
> *He trains thus: 'I shall breathe out experiencing joy.'*

This refers to the attainment of the first two jhānas (meditation stages of understanding).

The description of these stages is a set formula that is repeated many times in the suttas.[12]

We will now look into the description of these first two jhānas:

Here quite secluded from sensual pleasures, ...

When one starts their meditation session, they first close their eyes.

This is being secluded from the sensual pleasure of seeing.

When a sound distracts mind's attention, the instructions are to let the sound be there by itself, without thinking about whether the meditator likes the sound or not.

Simply 6R the sound and let it go, let go of the mental fist around the sound, relax the tightness in the head caused by that disturbance, feel mind become calm and at ease, smile, then redirect mind's attention back to the object of meditation, i.e., Loving-Kindness or the Breath.

The meditator stays with the breath or Loving-kindness and relaxes the tension and mind until the next distraction appears by itself, then they 6R again.

One does this with seeing, hearing, smelling, tasting, bodily sensations, and thoughts or any kind of sensual pleasure, which distracts mind away from the loving-kindness and relaxing or breath and relaxing.

The 6R's are the most useful tool to use all of the time in life.

The 6R's should become very automatic and happen by themselves by now.

Whenever there is a distraction of the sense-doors one must use the 6R's and let it go, relax that mental fist around the distraction - loosen the tightness in the head, open and expand mind, smile and redirect mind's attention back to the breath and relaxing or loving-kindness, and relaxing again.

It doesn't matter how many times the sensual pleasure arises.

The meditator has to allow it to be there every time it arises.

Just remember to 6R it and let it go, loosen the tightness in the head, feel mind expand, smile, and come back to the breath and relaxing or loving-kindness and relaxing.

secluded from unwholesome states

When mind is distracted from the breath and begins to think about feelings that arise, there is a tendency for mind to like or dislike that feeling.

This "thinking about" and "trying to control" arising feeling by thinking about it causes the feeling to get bigger and more intense.

Thus, the meditator causes even more pain or suffering to arise.

This mind/body process is made up of five different aggregates, which may or may not be affected by craving and clinging (conceptual thinking and opinions), depending on how sharp one's mindfulness is.

Some monks call them the clinging aggregates, but this is a bit misleading because it all depends on the meditator's mindfulness at the time.

If the object of meditation is not 6R-ed, then the aggregates affected by clinging will surely arise.

If the meditator's mindfulness remains keen and alert, then mind's attention will automatically stay on the object of meditation, they will be able to see the aggregates clearly as they truly are, and their mind's attention is not affected by craving and clinging at that time.

The meditator has a physical body (Kāya), feeling [vedanā] (both mental and physical), perception [saññā] (recognition, memory, and conceptualization), thoughts [saṅkhāra] (formations) and consciousness [viññāṇa].

By seeing this, one can clearly observe that feelings are one thing and thoughts are another.

Unfortunately, all of us have developed the habit of trying to think our feelings away.

This only makes the feelings bigger and more intense.

As a result, we cause ourselves so much more pain and suffering to arise.

When the meditator practices the Buddha's meditation method, they must understand and let go of this old habit of trying to "think" the feeling away.

Thus, when a feeling arises, no matter whether it is physical or emotional,

first, let go of that tight mental fist around the feeling;

now 6R it then relaxes the tightness in the head;

feel mind expand, then become calm and tranquil;

next the meditator lightly smiles;

then redirect mind's attention back to the breath and relaxing or mettā and relaxing.

When one does this, they are seeing the true nature of that feeling:

"It wasn't there—now it arose by itself—then it disappeared by itself," i.e. change or impermanence, this is unsatisfactory, and is completely impersonal.

By seeing the feeling, craving, clinging, habitual tendency, birth, sorrow, lamentation, pain, grief, and despair, the meditator is teaching themselves, HOW Dependent Origination actually arises and passes away.

The meditator certainly does not request for this incredibly painful sensation to arise, nor do they ask at that time to feel angry, sad, fearful, depressed, doubtful, or whatever the "catch of the day" happens to be.

Feeling arises by itself without the meditator's desire for it to arise.

A feeling lasts as long as it lasts and the meditator allows it to just be without keeping mind's attention on it.

If the meditator keeps mind's attention on any kind of distraction, they are feeding that distraction and it will grow from that kind of wrong effort.

The more the meditator tries to control an arising feeling, tries to fight with them, tries to push them away, or tries to make the feeling be the way the meditator wants it to be, then the more the unwanted feeling stays and becomes very much bigger and extra intense.

Why?

Because "who" wants this painful feeling to stop and go away?

"Who" wants the painful feeling to just leave and to stop bothering the meditator?

Of course the answer is "I" do!

"Who" wants to control the feeling with their thoughts?

Again, "I" do!

"Who" is trying to control their reality with concepts?

Again, "I" do!

Please remember that all thoughts are conceptual, we can't ever control reality by thinking it, because it only causes more and more suffering!

This happens not only with painful feeling; it happens with EVERY DISTRACTION THAT ARISES!

There is a great book that is highly recommended for serious meditation students, it is called *Concept and Reality* by Venerable Nanananda from Buddhist Publication Society.

This **marvel**ous book shows us that whenever one wants to control the feeling, they are identifying with that sensation or emotion as being theirs personally (attā). This kind of understanding, this expanded desire to control, is called Papañca in Pāli.

Whatever the meditator tends to think about i.e. how much it hurts, where did it come from, why does it have to bother them now, "Oh! I hate that feeling and want it to go away."

This is what happens when the meditator doesn't use the 6R's to gently let things go!

Every thought about the feeling is the ego-identification (attā) with that feeling.

Every time one tries to resist what is happening in the present moment, they are fighting with the **Dhamma of the Present Moment.**

When a painful or even a pleasant feeling arises, the Truth is—it is there!

Isn't that PROFOUND!

Any resistance, trying to control, wishing it away with thoughts, or fighting that feeling in any way, only causes more suffering to arise.

Actually whenever a feeling arises, one 6R's and opens mind—lets go of the want to control—then lovingly-accepts the fact that this feeling is there, and allows it to be there by itself.

Don't Resist Or Push; Smile and Soften This DROPSS is the key to having an accepting and open mind, which leads to the development of equanimity.

Any slightest resistance or tightness means that there is some ego-identification (attā) and craving still attached to it.

Let's say that a boss came up and scolded you in the early morning after you went to work.

What happened to your mind, at that time?

If you were like most people you took your bosses anger and made it your own anger, then scolded them back because you were angry.

- When the boss goes away, what do you think about?
- What you said, what your boss said;
- What you should have said;
- I'm right for feeling the way I do and for what I said;

- They are wrong for what they said and did;
- And so it goes!

This feeling of anger is strong and there are thoughts, which are attached to that feeling.

This is the way craving manifests.

After a little while you distract yourself with some other activities.

But the anger is still there and if someone comes to talk to you, chances are good that you will complain about your boss who scolded you.

At that time, you are passing along your craving, dissatisfaction, and anger to someone else and that affects them in a negative way.

At different times during the day, these feelings and the thoughts that you are attached to by craving and clinging arise.

As a matter of fact, these thoughts are just as if they were recorded on a cassette tape.

They come back in the same order and with exactly the same words.

After the end of the day you would have distracted yourself such that this feeling doesn't come up so often.

Then comes the time to sit in meditation and purify mind by 6Ring and learning how to let go of the craving.

But what arises?

This feeling of anger, and the associated thoughts!

This is the old habitual tendency coming up.

The habitual tendencies are called *Bhava* in Pāli, which arises right after clinging (conceptual thinking and opinions).

So, here we go again!

But this time, as you use the 6R's and let go of getting involved with those feelings and thoughts, you begin to let them go.

Seeing that these thoughts cause the feeling to grow, the meditator begins to soften mind.

"Never mind!" It just isn't that important." 6R → Relax → Soften→ "Let it be." → open mind and let go of that tight mental knot around these thoughts → let go of the aversion to the feeling → relax then feel mind begin to expand → now loosen the tightness in the head → feel mind become calm, what relief!

Now gently smile and go back to the breath → on the in-breath loosen the tightness in the head → on the out-breath relax the tightness in the head → always feeling mind open up, expand, become tranquil and clear.

Then the anger comes up again, and so again you do the same thing → 6R it → let it be there by itself without getting involved with the thinking about it →open and relax the mental hold of it → loosen the tightness in the head → softly smile and redirect mind's attention back to the breath and relax again.

This becomes the pattern of best practice to continue on with.

It doesn't matter how many times mind's attention goes back to that feeling of anger.

It is treated in the same way every time.

The meditator is not taking that feeling personally when they let the feeling be there by itself.

There is no ego-identification (anattā) with that feeling. This is seeing the true nature of that feeling, isn't it?

The feeling wasn't there before, but now it is. This is seeing impermanence (anicca).

When that feeling arises, it takes away the tranquility and peace. That was definitely painful, a true form of suffering (dukkha).

When one allows the feeling to be there by itself without getting involved or thinking about it, open their mind and relax the tightness away, they are experiencing the not-self (anattā) nature at that time.

When one practices Tranquil Wisdom Insight Meditation, they do experience the three characteristics of existence: impermanence, suffering, and not-self in the context of Dependent Origination.

As one continues to loosen mind's attention and let go of any distraction, the attachment (I am that!) becomes smaller and weaker.

Finally, it doesn't have enough strength to arise any more.

When this happens, mind becomes filled with relief and joy.

This letting go of attachment (craving) is **being secluded from unwholesome states.**

When one lets go and the joy arises, it lasts for a period of time.

As a result, mind's attention becomes very tranquil and peaceful.

The meditator experiences a mind, which is very comfortable (happiness) and stays on the object of meditation very easily.

When this is done repeatedly, mind will naturally become calm and composed by itself.

At that time, one begins to develop some equanimity and balance of mind.

The person enters upon and abides in the first Jhāna (meditation stage), which is accompanied by thinking and examining thought, with joy and happiness born of seclusion.

All of these different factors make up what is commonly called the first jhāna (meditation stage of understanding).

At that time there can still exist some very little wandering thoughts.

If mind's attention wanders away from the breath and relaxing, these wandering thoughts are noticed very quickly.

Lightly 6R then let go, relax the tightness, and smile before coming back to the breath and relaxing.

Some meditation teachers call this "access concentration."

But actually they are looking at things from the viewpoint of one-pointed concentration meditation and not Tranquil Wisdom Insight Meditation.

"Thinking and Examining Thought" are descriptions of the thinking mind and discursive thinking is wandering thoughts.

Some translations call initial and sustained thought as thinking and pondering.

There can still be directed thoughts in each one of the different jhānas (meditation stages of understanding).

The difference between directed thought and wandering thoughts is: With wandering thoughts, one thinks about what happened in the past or what will happen in the future, or daydream about what they would like to see.

Observation thought is about what is happening in the present moment.

These are observation thoughts, i.e., mind feels very happy right now, or mind is very calm and relaxed, and the body feels very still and peaceful right now, etc.

There is also another way of looking at "Thinking and Examining Thought,"

"Thinking" is mind that notices when mind is distracted and brings the attention back to the breath.

"Examining Thought" is mind that stays on the breath and relaxing without slipping away again and is continually examining whether mind's attention is beginning to wobble or vibrate away from the meditation object.

When mind begins to stay on the object of meditation for longer and longer periods of time, the relief and joy will become quite strong.

The meditator will naturally feel like smiling, because the joy is such a pleasurable feeling in both mind and body.

At that time, the body and mind feels very light until it is almost like floating.

This is quite a nice and pleasant experience.

Why? Because mind is free from craving and clinging at that time!

Some meditation teachers tell their students that when joy arises, *"Don't Be Attached!"*

Thus, these students become fearful of that joy and try to push it away so that they won't have the chance to possibly become attached.

However, this is not the correct thing to do because it doesn't matter what kind of feeling that arises, either pleasurable or painful or neutral, the meditator's job is to 6R that so mind's attention stays on the breath and opening then relaxing.

If mind's attention is pulled away by a feeling, simply let it be there by itself and relax the tightness in the head, feel mind open and expand, then gently smile and go back to the breath and relaxing.

Attachment or craving comes from getting involved with liking or disliking what arises in the present moment, whereas clinging is the thinking about it.

The Meditator will not become attached when they 6R and allow whatever arises to be there by itself.

After joy fades away, mind will become very calm, tranquil, peaceful and comfortable.

It is this comfortable and tranquil feeling that is called **"happiness born of seclusion."**

At first, one can sit in this stage of meditation for ten or fifteen minutes and longer with practice.

This is the first jhāna (meditation stage of understanding) and it will arise when the meditator has let go of sensual pleasure for a period of time, and has also let go of unwholesome habits or states (craving) of mind which stops the meditator from having a mind without distractions in it.

When the meditator has experienced this state of calm, they begin to realize the reasons why they are meditating.

At that time, mind's attention is nicely composed and happy with very few distractions.

There is more peace of mind than has ever been experienced before.

Thus, after that experience, one becomes enthusiastic and wants it to happen every time when they sit.

BUT, that very desire to have those calm states of mind is the very thing that stops them from arising!

The meditator then tries even harder and puts in more effort.

Unfortunately, mind only becomes more and more restless and unsettled.

This is due to restlessness and having the desire for something to happen in a particular way.

When it doesn't happen that way, the meditator pushes harder and tries to force things to be calm and tranquil.

In other words, the meditator is trying too hard and putting in wrong effort.

The meditator wants to control things and when mind doesn't co-operate, frustration sets in.

The question one needs to ask themselves at that time is:

"Who" wants something to be the way they want it to be?"

Of course the answer is always "I" do!

The next question to ask oneself is:

"Who" is trying to control their feelings with their thoughts and using extra effort to do this?"

Again the answer is "I" am!

So, now it is time to relax and laugh about who is in control!

Laughing is an amazing tool for the meditator, because when one laughs it changes our perspective to immediately come into Harmony with what is happening and the idea changes from "I" want this or "I" don't want that, to this is only "A" feeling!

Laughing helps the meditator to see clearly that they are attached and when this is seen clearly, it is easy to let go of it.

The meditator cannot experience this calm stage of meditation due to the attachment of wanting things to occur as they want (craving or tension and tightness in both mind and body).

This desire, which is in fact craving, causes the meditator to lean out of the present moment and to try to make the next present moment the way they want it to be!

When that present moment isn't right, they try even harder.

However, this calm state of mind will happen only when conditions are right.

Just relax, smile, and let go of that strong desire, calm down, and stop expecting things to work according to your own desires and attachments.

After the first experience of jhāna, mind may become quite active the next time the meditator sits in meditation.

But, if mindfulness is sharp, it will be able to quickly recognize when mind goes away.

Then they can let it go, open mind up, relax, smile, and return mind's attention back to the breath and relaxing.

Relaxing and opening on the in-breath; relaxing and loosening mind on the out-breath is what the Buddha instructs us to do.

Before long, mind's attention will settle down again and joy will arise again.

When joy fades away, the meditator will again experience that comfortable happy feeling, as well as a mind that is still and at ease.

At this time, the meditator still has the experience of all the five aggregates affected by craving and clinging.

If a meditator is practicing absorption concentration, they have no true awareness of these aggregates while they are in the absorption jhāna.

In the tranquility jhāna the meditator can still hear things or have feelings arise in the body.

For example, they would know when a mosquito lands on them.

The meditator may even have some thoughts about that mosquito, but they quickly recognize that this is a distraction and 6R it → let it go →relax → loosen the tension in the head and mind, relax, then softly smile and come back to the breath and relaxing.

As the meditator continues to relax, open, and calm mind on the in and out breath, eventually they will arrive at a stage where there are no more wandering thoughts.

The joy is a little stronger, and lasts a little longer. When it fades away, the comfortable feeling of happiness is stronger and the calm mind goes deeper into the breath and relaxing.

In the sutta, this state is described as:

> *Again with the stilling of applied and sustained thought, the person enters and abides in the second jhāna, which has self-confidence and stillness of mind without thinking and examining thought, with joy and happiness born of unified mind.*

The stilling of thinking and examining thought means that at that time, mind becomes very still and stays on the object of meditation quite nicely.

There is no discursive thinking about the past or future.

However, there can still be observation thoughts.

Remember that true meditation is silent, open observation, or "Noble Silence."

There is still feeling in the body, since all of the sense doors are working.

But, for example, if a sound arises, it doesn't make mind shake or move.

The meditator knows where they are and what they are doing.

The self-confidence mentioned in the sutta comes from the confidence one gains when they see clearly for themselves how well the meditation works.

Self-confidence not only arises when one is sitting in meditation, but also during the daily activities.

The stillness of mind means that mind is very calm and doesn't run around.

It is contented to stay on the breath and relax on the in and out breaths. These are the descriptions of the first two jhānas.

We now return to the Ānāpānasati Sutta.

> *He trains thus: 'I shall breathe in experiencing Happiness'; He trains thus: 'I shall breathe out experiencing happiness.'*

As the meditator continues with their practice, calming and opening mind in this way, eventually they reach a stage where the feeling of joy becomes too coarse and it naturally won't arise anymore.

This is always a rather comical time for the teacher, because the meditator comes to the teacher and says:

Student: There's something wrong with my meditation!

Teacher: Why do you say that?

Student: I don't feel any more joy,

Teacher: Is that bad?

Student: No, of course not, but still, why don't I feel any more joy?

Teacher: Do you feel comfortable and calmer than ever before? Does your mind have a strong sense of balance in it? Do you feel very much at ease?

Student: Yes, I feel all of that, but I don't feel any more joy!

Teacher: Good. Continue. Everything is going along just fine. Relax and stop demanding that joy arises when you want it to.

Student: But I like the joy. It makes me feel good!

Teacher: Who likes the JOY?

Student: Oh! Right! I got caught again, didn't I?

Teacher just smiles and says: Continue on!

The joy fades away by itself, and a very strong sense of balance and calm becomes quite apparent.

One can still hear sounds, and even though the body seems to disappear, at times one would know if someone were to touch them during their sitting meditation.

However, mind's attention does not move or get distracted by external things.

This is what it means when the sutta says the meditator has full awareness. It is described as:

> *Again, with the fading away of joy, a person abides in equanimity, and mindful and fully aware, still feeling happiness (or pleasure) with the body, he/she enters upon and abides in the third jhāna, on account of which noble ones announce: 'He has a pleasant abiding who has equanimity and is mindful.'*

With the description above, one can plainly see that being in the third jhāna, mind is very clear, alert and balanced.

The meditator is aware of what is happening around them, but mind's attention stays on the object of meditation easily and comfortably.

Being alert (being mindful) and having equanimity in mind is an unusual thing to experience because this state of meditation is the highest and best feeling that they have ever experienced in their whole life to this point!

Furthermore, one is not attached to it due to the gradually stronger equanimity that is arising.

At the same time, the body and mind are exceptionally relaxed and at ease.

What a nice state to be in!

This is why Noble Ones praise this state.

Besides this easing of the tightness in the head, the body loses tension, and the feeling of sensations begins to disappear.

This is because the tightness (craving) in mind causes tension (craving) in the body.

But now mind is so comfortable and tension free (craving-free) that the tension in the sensation of the body goes away too.

When this happens, the body becomes so soft and comfortable that there is no gross or big feeling arising in the meditator's body.

However, the meditator is aware when there is external contact like someone touching them.

This is the meaning of being "mindful and fully aware.".

Mind knows what is happening around it, but it just does not shake or become disturbed.

This is what one calls experiencing happiness on the in and out-breath and relaxing.

Some Fixed Concentration Meditation teachers say that when one is in this state of jhāna, the meditator can no longer experience the body or any of the sense doors and their mind is completely absorbed in a nimitta (sign).

They claim that the meditator will not know if someone were to hit them with a stick or someone were to change their positions of their hands and feet.

This is because their mind is so deeply absorbed into the object that they can't be fully aware of what is happening around them.

This is clearly not true, if one were to read the suttas or when practicing Tranquil Wisdom Insight Meditation.

> *He trains thus: 'I shall breathe in experiencing the mental formation'; he trains thus: 'I shall breathe out experiencing the mental formation'; He trains thus: 'I shall breathe in tranquilizing the mental formation.' He trains thus: 'I shall breathe out tranquilizing the mental formation.'*

As the meditator continues calming, expanding, and relaxing mind then smiling, mind's attention naturally begins to go deeper.

Finally, the feeling of pleasure in the body/mind becomes too coarse and mind experiences exceptional equanimity and balance of mind.

It is described thus in the suttas:

> *Here with the abandoning of pleasure and pain, and with the previous disappearance of joy and grief a monk enters upon and abides in the fourth jhāna (meditation stage), which has neither pain or pleasure and purity of mindfulness due to equanimity.*

When mind's attention becomes exceptionally calm and still, the meditator experiences deep tranquility and equanimity of mind.

The meditator can still hear sounds and feel sensations with the body when there is external contact, but these things do not shake or disturb mind at all.

Another description of this stage of understanding (jhāna) is:

The meditator's composed mind was purified, bright, unblemished, rid of imperfection, malleable, wieldy, steady and attained to imperturbability.

This gives the serious meditator an idea of what to expect when one attains this stage.

Mind's attention is exceptionally clear, bright, pure, and alert.

Mind's attention can even see when a distraction begins to arise, then 6R it, let it go, let it be and relax, open up, expand and calm down again and smile before coming back to the breath and relaxing.

In other words, the meditator practices the use of the 6R's.

The "abandoning of pain and pleasure" does not mean that occasionally pain or pleasure won't arise.

They will arise, but mind is in such a state of balance that it won't shake, wobble, or become involved with the distractions.

At that time mind is very aware when pain or pleasure arises but the equanimity and mindfulness is so strong that it does not become concerned with it.

The previous disappearance of joy and grief means the meditator's mind has let go of the lower emotional states of liking and disliking.

All of the stages of the lower jhāna involve letting go of emotional states of mind.

At first, when one begins to learn about meditation, they let go of very low coarse states, which frequently move mind's attention away from the meditation object.

After the meditator begins to learn how to calm mind, they can sit for longer periods of time without any distractions arising.

The meditator then experiences the thinking and examining applications of mind and the other jhāna factors.

When mind settles deeper, the thinking and examining application of mind disappears.

Joy becomes stronger for a while, but gradually it becomes too coarse and mind has too much movement in it.

Thus, mind will naturally go even deeper into the object of meditation and joy will fade away by itself.

At this time there is equanimity, happiness, mindfulness, and full awareness.

All these states of mind are very pleasant experiences.

But eventually, the happiness is too coarse a feeling and so mind goes deeper into the breath and at the same time, continues opening, expanding, and relaxing.

At this point the breath and the relaxing of mind begin to arise together.

The meditator notices that different parts of their body seem to disappear or are not felt unless the meditator directly puts their attention on those parts that have seemed to disappear.

Then, happiness fades away and all that remains in mind is strong equanimity, exceptional mindfulness, and composure of mind.

This is how the meditator experiences and tranquilizes the mental formations.

As Krishnamurti describes the true meditative state:

> A meditative mind is silent. It is not the silence, which thoughts can conceive of; it is not the silence of a still evening; it is the silence when thoughts, with all their images, words and perceptions have entirely ceased naturally. This meditative mind is the religious mind—the religion that is not touched by the church, the temples or by chanting.

20] He trains thus: 'I shall breathe in experiencing mind'; he trains thus 'I shall breathe out experiencing mind.'

At this time, the meditator's mind becomes very calm and any slight disturbance is noticed and let go of quickly and 6R'd easily.

First, mind lets go of tightness, now it goes back to the breath and relaxing, opening, expanding, and calming on the in-breath by relaxing, stretching out, and relaxing mind on the out-breath.

He trains thus: 'I shall breathe in gladdening mind'; he trains thus: 'I shall breathe out gladdening mind.'

When one reaches this stage of meditation, they begin to experience a finer and more exalted type of joy, which is described as the Joy (Pharana Pīti) Enlightenment Factor.

Mind becomes very peacefully content and at ease like never before.

This is called "gladdening mind" because it is such a pleasurable state to be in.

At that time, mind is exceptionally uplifted, very clear and mindfulness is sharper than ever before.

The equanimity is even more balanced and composed.

He trains thus: 'I shall breathe in stilling mind'; he trains thus: 'I shall breathe out stilling mind.'

At this time, mind becomes more subtle and calm, with very few distractions.

When they do arise, they are quickly noticed, let go of, calm mind, and return back to the breath and relaxing.

Naturally, the breath, the calming of mind, and smiling become easier and more serene.

They happen together naturally at the same time.

He trains thus: 'I shall breathe in liberating mind'; he trains thus: 'I shall breathe out liberating mind.'

Liberating mind means that the meditator stays on the breath with enough joyful interest that when mind's attention begins to move or go away from the breath and relaxing, they are aware and let the distractions go without any identifying or having any craving arise.

The meditator then 6R's, relaxes mind before coming back to the breath and relaxing on both the in and out-breath.

When a hindrance arises, one sees it quickly and lets it go without hesitation.

At this point sloth and torpor, or restlessness and anxiety, are the biggest obstacles to one's practice.

Whenever a hindrance arises, it will knock the meditator out of the jhāna and can cause all kinds of disturbances.

Please remember that the hindrance arises because the meditator's energy is out of balance with their composure of mind.

The phrase, liberating mind, also means to let go of the lower jhānas (meditation stages) and all of the jhāna factors by not being attached (thinking about and identifying with) them in any way.

He trains thus: 'I shall breathe in contemplating impermanence'; he trains thus: 'I shall breathe out contemplating impermanence.'

As one continues their practice of meditation on the breath and relaxing, plus calming and expanding mind, eventually mind becomes very deep and then they begin to notice that mind is expanding and getting bigger.

Silence and spaciousness of mind go together.

The immensity of silence is the immensity of mind in which a center point does not exist; basically speaking, at this time, there is no center and there is no outer edge.

The space continually grows and expands.

The meditator begins to see that there are no boundaries, and space and mind are infinite.

The Anupada Sutta, Sutta Number 111 in Majjhima
Nikāya, described this as:

*Again, by passing beyond gross perceptions of
form, by non-attraction to the gross
perceptions of change, aware that space is
infinite, the person enters into and abides in
the base of "infinite space".*

*And the states in the base of infinite space -
the perception of the base of infinite space
and the unification of mind. One still has the
five aggregates affected by craving and
clinging, the form, feelings, perception,
formations and mind.*

This added statement about the Five Aggregates is
interesting because the aggregates and the Four
Foundations of Mindfulness are actually one and the same
thing!

This, in turn, means that even while the meditator is in the
arūpa jhānas, if they are following the instruction precisely,
the meditator is keeping their Four Foundations going all of
the time!

There is full awareness and strong mindfulness in all of the
realms of the arūpa jhāna.

These are not states where the meditator loses awareness of
the breath or awareness of body!

To the contrary the meditator's mind becomes very highly
alert and attentive to what is happening around them, but
they don't re-act to external distractions.

They are aware of them but equanimity is so strong that
they don't distract mind's attention.

Now the meditator has moved out of the fine material jhāna (rūpa) stages and is beginning to experience the immaterial jhānas (arūpa jhāna).

Passing beyond gross perceptions of form means that even though one knows that they have a body at that time and when the meditator feels contact with an external object, they will absolutely know it.

This awareness would not readily pull mind's attention towards it because mind at that time is so deep in equanimity.

But they are still aware of the contact.

In this state of jhāna, the meditator is very aware of mind and what it is doing.

The "disappearance of all gross perceptions sense resistance and non-attraction to the gross perceptions of change" means even though a pain arises in the body, one knows it but does not get involved with that sensation.

At this time, the meditator feels mind growing, changing, and expanding, but they are not distracted from the breath or the relaxing of mind.

The meditator's mind is continually moving and expanding but their mind accepts this as it truly is.

Seeing impermanence in every link of Dependent Origination, seeing HOW the meditator's mind changes and expands, the meditator realizes that this phenomenon is part of an impersonal (anattā) process in which they have no control.

This is when the meditator begins to truly understand the impersonal (anattā) process of Dependent Origination and the Four Noble Truths and how they occur!

As the meditator continues on with the practice of opening and calming mind on the in-breath and the out-breath, they will eventually start to see consciousnesses arising and passing away.

They are continually coming up and going away, arising and passing away, without a break!

These consciousnesses keep coming into being, then vanishing in all the sense doors. This is described in the Anupada Sutta, section 13, as:

> *Again, by completely surmounting the base of" infinite space," aware that consciousness is infinite - a person enters upon and abides in the realm of" infinite consciousness."*
>
> *And the states in the base of" infinite consciousness"; - the perception of the base of infinite consciousness and the unification of mind.*
>
> *The meditator still has the five aggregates affected by craving and clinging, the bodily form, the feeling, perception, formations, and mind.*

When the meditator is in this state of "infinite consciousness," there can still arise some hindrances like torpor or dullness of mind, or restlessness.

These hindrances arise because the meditator's effort and attention which they put into their practice is out of balance with the rest of the enlightenment factors.

When there is too little energy, one experiences dullness (rarely does the meditator have sleepiness at this time).

On the other hand, if the meditator tries too hard or puts too much energy into the practice, restlessness will arise.

Both of these hindrances will knock the meditator out of the jhāna and they need to 6R the hindrance and also need to slightly adjust the amount of energy!

This fine-tuning will become very important as the meditator progresses in the meditation.

This state of "infinite consciousness" is like watching a moving picture when it is going too slowly.

Each individual consciousness is there for a brief moment and then passes away.

The meditator sees a blank spot in between each consciousness.

This occurs at each of the sense doors and it happens all of the time!

It happens when the meditator is doing their walking meditation, when the meditator is doing their daily activities, in short, all of the time!

When one is in this state, they see change happen so rapidly and continually, that it becomes very tiresome.

The meditator begins to see just how much un-satisfactoriness arises with each consciousness coming up and going away.

Thus, the meditator sees first hand impermanence, suffering, and they know that they have no control over these events.

These consciousnesses come up by themselves.

As a result, the meditator sees the impersonal (anattā) nature of these psycho-physical processes.

This is how one contemplates impermanence, by seeing how the process of Dependent Origination and the Four Noble Truths intertwine.

It is not done by thinking, but by direct experience and realizing it for oneself!

At this time the teacher will suggest that the meditator look at the space between the consciousnesses.

The student will begin to see the spaces more clearly and this leads to the below state.

We return to the Ānāpānasati Sutta.

> *He trains thus: 'I shall breathe in contemplating fading away'; he trains thus: 'I shall breathe out contemplating fading away.'*

As the meditator continues on with their practice on the in-breath, letting go and calming mind, and on the out-breath, letting go and calming mind, mind naturally let's go of observing all consciousnesses at each of the sense doors, which were so readily seen before.

Mind then gets into the realm of "nothingness."

This is when there is no external thing for mind to see.

There is mind looking at nothing outside of itself.

The Anupada Sutta says this:

> *Again, by completely surmounting the base of "infinite consciousness," aware that there is "nothing"; the meditator enters upon and abides in the "base of nothingness." And the states in the base of "nothingness";*

The perception of the base of nothingness and the unification of mind, again there are still the five aggregates affected by craving and clinging, the bodily form, feeling, perception, formations, and mind.

As odd as this may sound, it is an exceptionally interesting state to be in.

There are still many things to watch and observe, although there is nothing to see outside of mind and mental factors.

The meditator still has the Five Aggregates affected by craving and clinging, and some of the hindrances can still pop-up whenever one becomes either too lax or too energetic.

It is here that the Seven Awakening Factors become very important.

The Awakening Factors can be seen one by one as they occur.

When torpor arises, one must put mind back into balance by arousing the enlightenment factor of mindfulness, investigation of one's experience, energy, and joy.

If restlessness arises, one must sit without moving at all and arouse the enlightenment factors of mindfulness, tranquility, stillness, and equanimity. (More will be discussed later.)

At this time, mind's attention becomes very subtle and tricky.

It becomes extremely interesting to see the subtle ways it distracts one from meditation.

However, the meditator's mindfulness is quite strong and these tricks can be seen very easily.

The way the meditator closely observes is this:

- It's as if one were walking on a tight rope that is as thin as a spider's web.
- The meditator has to make very small adjustments in the amount of energy they use during the sitting, because mind's attention will continually change;
- And the meditator needs to *make these small adjustments* in the amount of energy they use during each sitting.

This is the time where the meditator will be able to sit comfortably for two or more hours at a time.

The meditator will be able to keep their meditation going when they get up and do their walking meditation.

The walking meditation will seem rather odd because it feels as if one's head is there, and there is nothing else felt except the bottoms of the feet where contact is made.

The thing to realize is one can experience even being in this deep jhāna state and still be doing their walking meditation.

He trains thus: 'I shall breathe in contemplating cessation'; he trains thus: 'I shall breathe out contemplating cessation.'

The meditator still continues on calming mind on the in and out breath.

At this time, mind begins to feel smaller and it seems to shrink.

Mind's attention becomes very subtle and still.

This is described in the Anupada Sutta as:

Again, by completely surmounting the base of nothingness, the person enters upon and

abides in the base of 'neither-perception nor non-perception (Neither feeling nor non-feeling and neither consciousness nor non-consciousness).

Mind's attention becomes so small and has such little movement that it is sometimes difficult to know whether there is a mind or not.

It is also difficult to know if there is any feeling, perception, or consciousness of mind.

This extremely fine state of mind is not easy to attain, yet it is attainable if one continues on with their practice of calming mind.

At this time, one cannot notice the breath any longer.

This is when one begins to sit for long periods of time. The 6R's are automatically occurring.

At this time, the meditation is the total tranquilizing and releasing of all energy and vibration.

The meditator begins to sit for two, three or four hours and this can be extended during retreats or at home with one's daily practice.

This is because it is such an interesting and quiet state to be in!

As the meditator continues on with their practice and keeps opening, expanding, and calming their mind, the subtlety becomes very fine and mind does not move or vibrate.

When the meditator comes out of this state, they reflect on what happened while they were in that state and they 6R every tiny thing that arises.

Eventually they will experience the state called Nirodha Samapatti or the Cessation of Perception, Feeling and Consciousness.

> *He trains thus: 'I shall breathe in contemplating relinquishment';*
> *he trains thus: 'I shall breathe out contemplating relinquishment.'*

This state of meditation is not the experience of the Supramundane Nibbāna yet, but it is very close at that time.

When the meditator comes out of this state of cessation, as consciousness returns, it is then that they will see very clearly all of the links of Dependent Origination (Paṭiccasamuppāda), both their arising and their ceasing. Only then does Nibbāna occur.

With the final letting go of ignorance, there are no more conditions and this is how the unconditioned state is realized.

This causes a huge shift in perspective and mind becomes totally dispassionate; it completely let's go of the belief in a permanent unchanging self or soul.

This is the only way one can experience the supramundane state of nibbāna, that is, by seeing directly all of the links of Dependent Origination, the Four Noble Truths, and the Three Characteristics of Existence.

This is why the experience is called the Doctrine of Awakening. The Anupada Sutta description is as follows:

> *Again, by completely surmounting the base of neither-perception nor non-perception, the person enters upon and abides in the cessation of perception, feeling and consciousness. And*

***his taints are destroyed, by his seeing with
wisdom.***

When one is in the state of the cessation of perception,
feeling and consciousness, they will not know that they are
in it. Why?

It is because they do not have any perception, feeling or
consciousness at all!

It is like all the lights were turned off on a very dark night.

At that time, one cannot see anything at all, not even if they
were to put their hands in front of their faces.

One may sit in this state for a period of time (maybe 5 or 10
or 15 minutes).

When the perception, feeling and consciousness comes
back, and the meditators mindfulness is sharp enough, they
will see and directly realize all of the Noble Truths!

When the meditator has seen all of the links of Dependent
Origination and the three characteristics of all existence in
each link, through this direct experience, they realize the
Third Noble Truth or the complete Cessation of Suffering!

The meditator automatically sees, understands and realizes
this.

It does not matter whether they have studied the links of
Dependent Origination or not, because the meditator has
developed the insights and understanding of HOW each
link arises and passes away by themselves.

This is where direct knowledge comes in. This is not
something that can be memorized or studied knowledge.

The statement: "And his taints are destroyed by his seeing with wisdom" indicates the direct observation of all of the Noble Truths directly.

In the texts, it repeatedly says, "when one sees Dependent Origination, they see the Dhamma and One who sees the Dhamma sees Dependent Origination."

This confirms the importance of the Knowledge and Vision (knowing by seeing) approach that the Buddha taught.

Thus, seeing Dependent Origination directly means that one sees and realizes all of the Noble Truths. This is how one contemplates relinquishment.

22] Monks that is how mindfulness of breathing is developed and cultivated, so that it is of great fruit and great benefit"

Fulfillment of the Four Foundations of Mindfulness

23] And how, monks, does mindfulness of breathing, developed and cultivated, fulfill the Four Foundations of Mindfulness?

24] Monks, on whatever occasion a person, breathing in long, understands: 'I breathe in long,' or breathing out long understands: 'I breathe out long'; Breathing in short, understands: 'I breathe in short,' or breathing out short, understands: 'I breathe out short':

The *"on whatever occasion"* is very interesting and has far reaching implications.

"On whatever occasion" does not mean only while sitting in meditation, but all of the time!

For instance, the Venerable Sāriputta was fanning the Buddha while he was giving a Dhamma talk to someone.

Ven. Sāriputta heard and observed the Buddha and got the realization that he was still having one more attachment.

Venerable Sāriputta was attached to the understanding he had gained by seeing how Dependent Origination actually occurred.

Then Venerable Sāriputta realized that the Buddha was not even attached to the Dhamma!

With that realization Venerable Sāriputta let go of this subtle attachment and in the "blink of an eye" he became an arahat with both the path knowledge and its fruition knowledge!

During the meditator's daily activities, when mind becomes heavy and full of thoughts, the meditator notices it, simply practices the 6R's.

Let go of the thoughts, calms and relaxes the tightness in mind, feels mind expand, then re-smiles lightly and mind becomes tranquil, then goes back to the breath and relaxing for one or two breaths.

This will help greatly in calming mind and to improve our mindfulness during one's daily activities.

Also, the meditator begins to smile into everything they do, because smiling helps to remind one to be more observant and happy!

This use of the 6R's is definitely a practical way to practice one's daily activities and improve their awareness of states of consciousness.

Every time the meditator does this during their daily activities, it brings a kind of awareness and lighter perspective into their lives.

It becomes easier to see the three characteristics of existence, impermanence, suffering, and the impersonal nature, while observing HOW Dependent Origination actually occurs even while working or playing.

The statement, **"On whatever occasion"** extends into one's walking meditation as well.

Instead of putting the attention on one's feet (as some meditation teachers recommend), the meditator can still keep their attention on mind, relaxing on the in and out breath, and of course smiling, while walking.

This is mindfulness of body and this can even extend into all other daily activities.

Mindfulness of mind objects is a very important aspect to be aware of and is much easier to watch than the physical body.

It is easy to recognize when mind's attention is tight and tense.

At that time the meditator can practice their 6R's, relax, loosen the tightness in the head, come back for one or two breaths, if they do not have time to do more right then and always continue smiling.

Remember: The first and second verses in the Dhammapada tell us *"Mind is the forerunner of all (good and bad) states. Mind is chief; mind-made are they."*

Everything follows mind's attention, be it happiness or suffering.

By comparison, in some other practices, to follow all the movements of the body very closely, a meditator would not be able to see mind clearly enough to realize the tightness caused by that movement of mind's attention.

Thus, directly being aware of mind's attention and all of its movements and tendencies to tighten was what the Buddha intended for the meditator to observe, when he said "On any occasion"

He trains thus: 'I shall breathe in experiencing the whole body'; He trains thus: 'I shall breathe out experiencing the whole body:

He trains thus: 'I shall breathe in tranquilizing the bodily formation'; He trains thus: 'I shall breathe out tranquilizing the bodily formation'

On that occasion a person abides contemplating the body as a body, ardent, fully aware, and mindful, having put away covetousness and grief for the world. I say that this is a certain body among the bodies, namely, in-breathing and out-breathing. That is why on that occasion a person abides contemplating the body as a body, ardent, fully aware, and mindful, having put away covetousness and grief for the world.

The statements about experiencing the whole body, and the tranquilizing of the bodily formations have already been discussed.

Thus, we won't repeat that section here.

Contemplating the body as a body is self-explanatory about the breath and relaxing.

Being ardent means working hard, or being ever alert.

This practice is actually very simple to do but it is sometimes not easy!

The phrase "fully aware and mindful" pertains to the alertness of mind when it is in the jhāna as well as during the daily activities.

When the meditator is in the "tranquility–insight jhāna" (samatha/vipassanā, TWIM), they are very aware of what is happening around them and their mindfulness is sharp and clear.

The meditator has no distracting thoughts to pull their attention away from the present moment.

When they use the 6R's, happiness increases and suffering diminishes.

The meditator is able to observe all mind states, feelings, sensations or distractions as well as the jhāna factors when they arise in mind, i.e., the joy, happiness, equanimity, stillness of mind, the calm composure of mind etc.

"Having put away covetousness and grief for the world" means mind has gone beyond the simple liking and disliking of distractions, emotions, painful feeling, pleasant feeling, happy feeling, and the thinking about them.

It means to let go of attachment to things, which cause suffering to arise.

The rest of the paragraph is just repeating that the breath meditation is part of mindfulness of breathing, and that it conforms with the First Foundation of Mindfulness of the Body.

25] Monks, on whatever occasion, a person trains thus: 'I shall breathe in experiencing joy'; they train thus: 'I shall breathe out experiencing joy';

They train thus: I shall breathe in experiencing happiness'; they train thus: 'I shall breathe out experiencing happiness';

They train thus: '1 shall breathe in experiencing the mental formation'; they train thus: 'I shall breathe out experiencing the mental formation';

They train thus: 'I shall breathe in tranquilizing the mental formation'; they train thus: 'I shall breathe out tranquilizing the mental formation'

This is again a repetition of the previous statement, and thus, we will continue without further delay.

On that occasion a person abides contemplating feeling as feeling, ardent, fully aware, and mindful, having put away covetousness and grief for the world. I say that this is a certain feeling among feelings, namely, giving close attention to the in-breathing and out-breathing. That is why on that occasion a person abides contemplating feeling as feeling, ardent, fully aware and mindful, having put away covetousness and grief for the world.

This describes all kinds of feeling, which occur when the meditator is in the meditation stages of the first four jhānas (levels of understanding).

It also says that the most important feeling among these feelings is the in and out breath.

This is because the meditator gets to experience the different stages of meditation.

If the meditator stops being attentive to the in and out breath and relaxing, their meditation progress stops.

The importance of staying with the in and out breath and relaxing cannot be understated.

This is how the Second Foundation of Mindfulness of Feeling is fulfilled.

26] Monks, on whatever occasion a person trains thus: 'I shall breathe in experiencing mind';
they train thus: 'I shall breathe out experiencing mind';

They train thus: 'I shall breathe in gladdening mind'; they train thus: 'I shall breathe out gladdening mind';

They train thus: 'I shall breathe in stilling mind'; they train thus: 'I shall breathe out stilling mind';

They train thus: 'I shall breathe in liberating mind'; they train thus: 'I shall breathe out liberating mind'.

This is again repetitive material. Please refer back to the other section for explanation.

On that occasion a person abides contemplating mind as mind, ardent, fully aware, and mindful, having put away covetousness and grief for the world.

I do not say that there is development of mindfulness of breathing for one who is forgetful, who is not fully aware.

That is why on that occasion a person abides contemplating mind as mind, ardent, fully aware, and mindful, having put away covetousness and grief for the world.

The statement, "I do not say there is development of mindfulness of breathing for one who is forgetful, who is not fully aware" is one of the strongest statements made in this sutta.

The function of mindfulness is to remember.

To remember what?

To remember to observe and to stay with the meditation object with joyful interest, and seeing clearly how mind's attention moves from one thing to another with clear comprehension.

When the meditator is in the "Tranquility/Insight jhāna" (samatha/vipassanā or TWIM), mind's attention becomes extraordinarily clear, bright, and alert.

As the meditator goes higher and higher along the path, more profound states of mind present themselves.

Mindfulness and full awareness becomes so refined that even the slightest movement of mind's attention can be observed, 6R'ed, and let go of.

Mind's attention becomes fluid, more expanded, spacious and free from tension, and the breath becomes clearer and easier to watch.

The meditator's attention begins to be unwavering and mind develops more composure than ever before.

This is how the Third Foundation of Mindfulness of Consciousness is fulfilled.

27] Monks, on whatever occasion

a person trains thus: 'I shall breathe in contemplating impermanence';
They train thus: 'I shall breathe out contemplating impermanence';

They train thus: 'I shall breathe in contemplating fading away';
they train thus: 'I shall breathe out contemplating fading away';

They train thus: 'I shall breathe in contemplating cessation';
They train thus: 'I shall breathe out contemplating cessation';

They train thus: 'I shall breathe in contemplating relinquishment';
They trains thus: 'I shall breathe out contemplating relinquishment'

This again is referring to the immaterial jhāna (arūpa jhāna), and how the meditator experiences the attainment of the Supramundane Nibbāna.

This sutta teaches the meditator how to reach all of the meditation stages of understanding and to attain the highest bliss.

Through realizing that all of the Four Noble Truths are seen and comprehended by observing HOW Dependent Origination arises and passes away and through the Fulfillment of the Four Foundations of Mindfulness and the Seven Awakening Factors, they relinquish all attachments (craving).

> *On that occasion a person abides contemplating mind-objects as mind-objects, ardent, fully aware, and mindful, having put away covetousness and grief for the world.*
>
> *Having seen with wisdom the abandoning of covetousness and grief, he closely looks on with equanimity. That is why on that occasion a person abides contemplating mind-objects as mind-objects, ardent, fully aware, and mindful, having put away covetousness and grief for the world.*

The phrase **'Having seen with wisdom'** is very interesting because anytime the word wisdom (or wise) is used it is always referring to understanding HOW the impersonal process of Dependent Origination occurs.

When the meditator experiences the higher jhāna (meditation stages of understanding), their mind's attention develops a finer and finer balance in it.

The meditator then experiences the **"abandoning of covetousness and grief, he closely looks on with equanimity."**

The meditator sees clearly how tricky mind truly is, and they keep a sense of equanimity in it, even though some unpleasant things may arise.

The true balance of meditation is learned when the meditator goes into the immaterial realms of jhāna.

This is when there is a real letting go (6Ring) of mental concepts, opinions, ideas, stories about, and attachments.

Mind's attention develops such a beautiful equanimity that even when the most unpleasant feelings arise, mind will accept it without being disturbed.

This is how the **Fourth Foundation of Mindfulness of Mind-Objects is fulfilled.**

28] Monks, that is how Mindfulness of Breathing, developed and cultivated, fulfills the Four Foundations of Mindfulness.

Fulfillment of the Seven Awakening Factors

29] And how, monks, do the Four Foundations of Mindfulness, developed and cultivated, fulfill the Seven Awakening Factors?

30] Monks, on whatever occasion a person abides contemplating the body as a body, ardent, fully aware, and mindful, having put away covetousness and grief for the world

on that occasion unremitting mindfulness (sati) is established in him.

On whatever occasion unremitting mindfulness is established in a person on that occasion mindfulness awakening factor is aroused in him, and he develops it, and by development, it comes to fulfillment in him.

Let us use a description from the Satipaṭṭhāna Sutta for more clarification. It says:

Here, there being mindfulness awakening factor (sati-bojjhaṅga) in him, a person understands:

'There is mindfulness awakening factor in me';

or there being no mindfulness awakening factor in him, he understands:

'There is no mindfulness awakening factor in me';

and he also understands how there comes to be the arising of the unarisen mindfulness awakening factor

and how the arisen mindfulness awakening factor comes to fulfillment by development.

This is rather straightforward. It simply says that one knows when their mind is silent, sharp, clear, and joyfully interested in the breath and relaxing.

The meditator also knows when mindfulness is dull, not sharp, and mind tends to be a little bored or disinterested.

When that happens, the meditator knows that they must pick-up their interest and see how everything that arises is truly different.

One then sees how every breath is different, never exactly the same.

This is how mindfulness awakening factor comes to fulfillment by development.

> *31] Abiding thus mindful, he investigates and examines that state with wisdom and embarks upon a full inquiry into it.*
>
> *On whatever occasion, abiding thus mindful, a person investigates and examines that state with wisdom and embarks upon a full inquiry into it –*
>
> *– on that occasion the investigation-of-states awakening factor (dhammavicaya bojjhaṅga) is aroused in him, and he develops it, and by development it comes to fulfillment in him.*

It is a very important to be familiar with the factor of investigation of one's experience.

The meditator takes a true interest in HOW things arise.

One must always use the 6R's rather than get caught in the conceptual process of thinking about why the distraction arose.

The content and reasons why distractions arise is of no concern to the Buddhist meditator.

The meditator must closely see HOW the process of Dependent Origination works in order to know it as an impersonal process.

This means whatever arises, whether it is any of the five hindrances, an emotional state, or a physical feeling, the meditator impersonally examines the process with interest.

This is done by not getting involved with thinking about the arising phenomena, but rather 6R-ing and observing it, allowing the distraction to be there, then letting it go mentally.

Next, the meditator relaxes that tight mental fist which hardily grabs the distraction, relaxes one time.

Loosening the tightness in mind/head/body, i.e. letting go of the craving, smiling, and redirecting mind's attention back to the breath and relaxing is what needs to be done.

Every time mind's attention is pulled away from the object of meditation, the meditator tries to see clearly the different aspects about that distraction.

Then 6R it, let it go, relax mind, smile and come back to the breath and relax again.

In this way, the meditator becomes more familiar with the distraction and is able to recognize it more quickly.

This type of investigation is described in the Satipaṭṭhāna Sutta as:

> *Here, there being the investigation-of-experience awakening factor (dhammavicaya bojjhaṅga) in them, a person understands: 'There is the investigation-of-experience awakening factor in me';*
>
> *or there being no investigation-of-experience awakening factor in them, a person understands: 'There is no investigation-of-experience awakening factor in me';*

and they also understand how there comes to be the arising of the unarisen investigation-of-experience awakening factor;

and how the arisen investigation-of-experience awakening factor comes to fulfillment by development.

In order to bring forth the awakening factor of investigation-of-experience, the meditator has to take a strong interest in HOW everything works according to the impersonal process of Dependent Origination.

The more the meditator examines their experiences, the easier it is to recognize all of the different and unusual aspects about the hindrances and distractions due to pain or emotional upset.

When the meditator sees these things clearly, it is much easier to let go of them.

It is also important to develop the perspective that this is an impersonal process, which is unsatisfactory and is always changing.

This perspective enables the meditator's practice to progress without periods of unclarity.

32] In one who investigates and examines that state with wisdom and embarks upon a full inquiry into it, tireless energy is aroused.

On whatever occasion tireless energy is aroused in a person who investigates and examines that state with wisdom and embarks upon a full inquiry into it –

- on that occasion the energy awakening factor is aroused in them, and they develop it, and by development it comes to fulfillment in them.

It takes a lot of energy and effort when the meditator takes sincere interest into HOW Dependent Origination occurs in the present moment and examines it with care.

As the meditator uses their energy and has a strong joyful interest, this causes even more energy to arise.

This is described in the Satipaṭṭhāna Sutta as:

Here, there being the energy awakening factor (vīriya bojjhaṅga) in him, a person understands: 'There is the energy awakening factor in me'; or there being no energy awakening factor in them, they understand:

'There is no energy awakening factor in me';

and he also understands how there comes to be the arising of the unarisen energy awakening factor

and how the arisen energy awakening factor comes to fulfillment by development.

33] In one who has aroused energy, unworldly joy arises

Unworldly joy (ubbega pīti) refers to joy that is experienced while in one of the first two jhānas

There is also the finer and higher type of joy, which is called the all-pervading joy (pharana pīti), which can be felt in all of the higher jhāna.

These are called "unworldly," because it has nothing at all to do with any sense pleasures, that is, the eye, ear, nose, tongue, or body.

> *On whatever occasion unworldly joy arises in a person who has aroused energy –*
>
> *– on that occasion the joy awakening factor (pīti bojjhaṅga) is aroused in them, and they develop it, and by development it comes to fulfillment in them.*

As one has attentive energy in staying on the breath, their mindfulness becomes sharper and their energy increases little by little.

When this happens, mind becomes quite happy and delights in staying on the breath, relaxing mind, smiling, and body.

This happy feeling has some excitement and is called "uplifting joy" (ubbega pīti).

There is another type of joy, which arises in the higher meditation states, and this is called the all-pervading joy (pharana pīti).

It doesn't have so much excitement and is very nice and cooling to mind.

These states of mind are not to be feared or pushed away.

It is a natural process when one develops and progresses along with their practice of meditation.

If the meditator stays on the breath and their mind's attention with interest and they do not get involved in enjoying the joy, no problems will arise.

But, if the meditator does happen to get involved with the joy, it will go away very quickly.

As a result, they will most likely experience sleepiness or sloth and torpor. The Ānāpānasati Sutta says:

> *Here, there being the joy awakening factor (pīti-bojjhaṅga) a person understands:*
>
> *'There is the joy awakening factor in me;*
>
> *or there being no joy awakening factor in them, they understand:*
>
> *'There is no joy awakening factor in me';*
>
> *and they also understand how there comes to be the arising of the un-arisen joy awakening factor,*
>
> *and how the arisen joy awakening factor comes to fulfillment by development.*

These first four awakening factors are very important when one experiences sloth and torpor.

Sloth means sleepiness and torpor means dullness of mind.

When one gets into the fourth jhāna and above, the two main hindrances, which arise are restlessness and torpor.

However, when one brings up the investigation factor of awakening and examines this torpor, they have to use more energy and this helps to overcome this dullness.

When one gets into the higher jhāna they must learn to fine-tune their practice little by little.

By being familiar with these awakening factors, the meditator will learn how to eventually balance all of the factors.

This directly leads to the supramundane state of Nibbāna.

The most important key for success in meditation is the first enlightenment factor of mindfulness.

Without mindfulness and the 6R's (right effort), one cannot possibly reach any of these meditation stages.

Mindfulness and the 6R's are the main keys to overcome both sloth and torpor, and restlessness.

Remember these hindrances can come at any time and knock the meditator right out of any of the meditation stages, even up to the realm of neither-perception nor non-perception (Neither feeling nor non-feeling, Neither consciousness nor non-consciousness).

Thus, the meditator must be very careful to recognize these awakening factors and skillful in learning how to use them when it is appropriate.

The next three awakening factors are important to overcome restlessness.

34] In one who is joyful, the body and mind become tranquil. On whatever occasion the body and mind become tranquil in a person who is joyful...

On that occasion the tranquility awakening factor (passaddhi bojjhaṅga) is aroused in them, and they develop it, and by development it comes to fulfillment in him.

When joy arises in mind, one feels very pleasant feelings in body and mind.

This is true, even in the higher stages of meditation, like the immaterial states of jhāna.

After a while, the joy fades a little and one's mind becomes exceptionally calm and peaceful.

This state is called the Awakening Factor of Tranquility.

At that time, the meditator's body and mind become extraordinarily peaceful and calm. The Ānāpānasati Sutta describes it thus:

> *Here, there being the tranquility awakening factor (passaddhi bojjhaṅga) in him, a person understands:*
>
> *'There is the tranquility awakening factor in me';*
>
> *or there being no tranquility awakening factor in them, they understand,*
>
> *'There is no tranquility awakening factor in me';*
>
> *and they also understand how there comes to be the arising of the unarisen tranquility awakening factor*
>
> *and how the arisen tranquility awakening factor comes to fulfillment by development.*

Actually, the strongest part of the tranquility awakening factor is the mental feeling.

It is a very nice, calm feeling of strong peace.

This is especially noticed when one is experiencing the first three immaterial jhāna, which are the "realm of infinite space," "the realm of infinite consciousness," and "the realm of nothingness."

*35] In one whose body is tranquil and who
feels pleasure, mind becomes still and
composed.*

*On whatever occasion mind becomes still and
composed in a person whose body is tranquil
and who feels pleasure - on that occasion the
collectedness awakening factor (samādhi
bojjhaṅga)*

This is frequently called the "concentration enlightenment
factor," but this term is too misunderstood. So the author
prefers to use "collectedness enlightenment factor."

*is aroused in them, and they develop it, and
by development it comes to fulfillment in
them.*

As the meditator's mind and body become more tranquil
and at ease, mind's attention stays on the breath and
relaxing more naturally, without any distractions.

It is much easier to open, relax mind, and smile with each
in and out breath.

Mind's attention is definitely composed and unruffled by
any internal or external distractions.

There comes a time when mind prefers to stay still on the
meditation object without force or trying to concentrate.

Mind's attention stays on the breath, relaxing and smiling
for very long periods of time now.

Of course, at this time, there is very sharp mindfulness and
full awareness.

The meditator still has full awareness even when they reach
the "realm of nothingness."

Mind's attention does not waver or move away from the breath, relaxing and smiling even though one hears sounds or knows that a mosquito has landed on them.

Mindfulness of breathing and stillness are very sharp and clear which will continue on for long periods of time.

When one is in the "realm of nothingness," they can explore and watch many different aspects of mind.

This can be called the "action of silence."

When mind is absolutely silent, it is the blessing that everyone is seeking.

In this collectedness, this quality of silence is perfection of the present moment. The Ānāpānasati Sutta describes this as:

> *Here, there being the collectedness awakening factor (samādhi bojjhaṅga) in him, a person understands:*
>
> *'There is the collectedness awakening factor in me';*
>
> *or there being no collectedness awakening factor in them, they understand:*
>
> *'There is no collectedness awakening factor in me';*
>
> *and they also understand how there comes to be the arising of the unarisen collectedness awakening factor*
>
> *and how the arisen collectedness awakening factor comes to fulfillment by development.*

36] He closely looks on with equanimity at mind thus stilled and composed.

On whatever occasion a person closely looks on with equanimity at mind thus stilled and composed –

on that occasion the equanimity awakening factor (upekkhā bojjhaṅga) is aroused in them, and they develop it, and by development it comes to fulfillment in them.

The equanimity awakening factor is again a very important factor to develop.

It keeps mind's attention balanced even when one's attention becomes unsettled.

The equanimity awakening factor is the only factor which allows mind to lovingly-accept whatever arises in the present moment.

For example, if there arises any kind of pain (physical or emotional), it doesn't distract the meditator.

The equanimity awakening factor is the factor which helps one to see things impersonally and without the ego-identification of getting involved with distractions.

It is the seeing of what arises in the present moment with complete balance.

The seeing and understanding of anattā (not-self) is the very thing which allows the meditator to progress rapidly along the Buddha's Path.

But the meditator must be somewhat careful with this equanimity because it is often mistaken to be indifference.

Indifference has some dissatisfaction, aversion, and a lack of mindfulness in it, but equanimity does not.

Equanimity has only openness, sharp mindfulness, and complete acceptance of everything that arises in the present moment.

Equanimity opens mind totally and significantly shifts the meditator's perspective so they see everything as being an impersonal process.

Indifference closes mind and tries to ignore what is happening in the present moment.

The Ānāpānasati Sutta describes it thus:

Here, there being the equanimity awakening factor (upekkhā bojjhaṅga) in him, a person understands:

'There is the equanimity awakening factor in me';

or there being no equanimity awakening factor in them, they understand:

'There is no equanimity awakening factor in me';

and they also understand how there comes to be the unarisen equanimity awakening factor

and how the arisen equanimity awakening factor comes to fulfillment by development.

These last three awakening factors, tranquility, collectedness, and equanimity will greatly assist the meditator when restlessness arises in mind.

Restlessness makes mind think many thoughts and causes lots of unpleasant feelings to arise in the body.

As a result, the meditator feels like breaking the meditation and distracting themselves in one way or another.

To say the least, it is a very hard mind that causes suffering to be more noticeable.

The only way to overcome restlessness is by developing stillness of mind and tranquility of body along with strong equanimity.

When mind has restlessness in it, there is no balance of mind at all, mind is very distracted.

Instead, there is a lot of ego-identification (attā) with that terrible feeling.

To overcome this hindrance, one has to allow it to be there by itself and still mind.

By bringing forth the stillness, tranquility, and equanimity awakening factors and focusing mind on these different factors, the meditator will overcome the restlessness.

The two major hindrances that always seem to trouble meditators are torpor, or dullness of mind, and restlessness or over activity of mind.

The meditator had better become friends with these two hindrances, because they will stay around until they become an arahat.

Thus, the sooner we drop all resistance to these states when they arise and begin to explore them with joyful interest, the faster we will be able to recognize them.

As a result, we will be able to let these hindrances go faster and return into the jhāna.

37] Monks, on whatever occasion a person abides contemplating feeling as feeling, ardent, fully aware, and mindful, having put away covetousness and grief for the world on that occasion unremitting mindfulness is established in him.

On whatever occasion unremitting mindfulness is established in a person, the equanimity awakening factor is aroused in him, he develops it, and by development it comes to fulfillment in him.

The meditator must 6R and realize that whenever any hindrance or distraction arises, they must use these awakening factors,

It does not matter if the hindrance arises during sitting meditation or during daily activities.

These factors put mind back in balance whenever a distraction bumps it.

This continues through all of the Four Foundations of Mindfulness.

It shows the meditator how to use the Seven Awakening Factors at all times while practicing Mindfulness of Breathing meditation.

These awakening factors do arise one by one as they occur and not all at the same time.

Also, it shows the importance of jhāna in relationship to the development of mind and how there is great fruit and great benefit to be enjoyed when we follow these simple instructions.

38] Monks, on whatever occasion a person contemplates mind as mind, ardent, fully aware, and mindful, having put away covetousness and grief for the world. - on that occasion unremitting mindfulness is established in him.

On whatever occasion unremitting mindfulness is established in a person, the equanimity awakening factor is aroused in them, and they develop it, and by development it comes to fulfillment in him.

39] Monks, on whatever occasion a person abides contemplating mind-objects as mind-objects, ardent, fully aware, and mindful, having put away covetousness and grief f6r the world - on that occasion unremitting mindfulness is established in him.

On whatever occasion unremitting mindfulness is established in a person, the equanimity awakening factor is aroused in them, and they develop it, and by development it comes to fulfillment in them.

40] Monks that is how the Four Foundations of Mindfulness, developed and cultivated, fulfill the Seven Enlightenment Factors.

When the Seven Awakening Factors are in perfect balance, the potential of attaining the Supramundane Nibbāna occurs.

As the meditator goes higher and higher in the jhāna, the balance of the awakening factors becomes finer and much subtler.

This fine-tuning of mind's attention becomes so interesting that the meditator is naturally inclined to sit for much longer periods of time.

This meditation is by far the best show in town!

Some meditators get up very early in the morning so that they have enough time to watch and learn the balance of mind and still go to work.

This meditation turns out to be the most gratifying and fun exploration that anyone can ever experience in life.

Fulfillment of True Knowledge and Deliverance

41] And how, monks, do the Seven Awakening Factors, developed and cultivated, fulfill true knowledge and deliverance?

42] Here, monks, a person develops mindfulness awakening factor, which is supported by seclusion, dispassion, and cessation, and ripens in relinquishment.

The term "supported by seclusion" means that one must, at least, gain the first jhāna.

As was stated above, the description of the first jhāna starts with **"to be secluded from sensual pleasure, then to be secluded from unwholesome states."**

At that time, mind is alert and stays on the object of meditation with clarity, i.e. no distractions.

If a distraction begins to arise, mindfulness recognizes it and lets it go and relaxes.

Next, the description says the happiness experienced comes about by being born of seclusion.

This is how one's mindfulness awakening factor is supported by seclusion.

Dispassion means mind is free from attachments, craving and clinging, i.e., not thinking or analyzing.

Gaining the fourth jhāna means to reach a stage of having an imperturbable mind; a mind that has such strong equanimity, it is impossible to be disturbed and in this way mind becomes dispassionate.

This is how the meditator's mindfulness awakening factor is supported by dispassion.

Cessation here means the ceasing of defilements and ego-identification (attā) with what arises.

It means that the meditator has let go of craving.

"Being mindful" is a term that, in the past, has always had a kind of slippery meaning and it is not what most people think.

It's meaning is very simple and precise when seen as 'remembering to observe the movements of mind's attention' or remembering to have strong alertness.

Being truly mindful means we are aware at all times of what mind is doing; that we are able to let go of the things that cause tension to arise in the head, relax, and tranquilize both body and mind.

It includes observing how this whole process works and allows it to just be, without getting involved in the drama of things.

Not getting involved with the drama of things means not to identify with, or take personally this impersonal process or try to control the present moment.

"Being mindful" means "to lovingly open one's mind and let go of all identification with that distraction, then relax the tension in the head and mind," so that one can see things clearly and calmly.

Whenever the meditator tries to resist or control what is happening in the present moment, at that time, they are fighting with the Dhamma or the Truth of the Present Moment.

This fighting with the reality of the moment causes much unsatisfactoriness and suffering to arise.

This is what the Dhammapada refers to as "seeing what is essential as being essential and what is unessential as being unessential."

However, when the meditator is mindful and sees clearly that this is just a phenomena arising and passing away, they can open up and accept it, without hardening mind or resisting in any way.

At this time, **joyful interest** is very important because when mind has some joy in it there is no anger, jealousy, aversion, fear, or anxiety.

Joyful interest helps the meditator to have the proper perspective of seeing what happens in the moment impersonally (anattā).

When mind's attention is uplifted, the meditator more easily sees that whatever arises is just part of a continuing process which they can learn from.

Joy causes mind to be uplifted, which is why it is an awakening factor and very important to one's practice.

Also, when joy is in the meditator's mind, they are pleasant to be around.

Remember, the acronym that is very helpful to use is *DROPSS.*

It stands for *Don't Resist Or Push, Smile and Soften* mind and helps us to accept everything when it occurs, because that is the "Dhamma of the Moment."

When the meditator continues on with the practice, their mind will eventually attain to the higher and more subtle stages of meditations (arūpa jhāna).

At that time, the meditator's mind can experience the realm of "nothingness.".

This is what is called cessation.

It is called **nothingness** because **there is nothing more to watch outside of mind.**

When the meditator experiences the realm of "nothingness," their mind is watching nothing.

But, mind is still there and the different awakening factors can arise along with the five aggregates, which *may* be affected by craving and clinging.

Also, some hindrances can still arise and knock the meditator out of that surpassed state of immaterial jhāna.

Thus, there is nothing for mind to watch outside of itself, and yet there is still lots to see and understand about HOW mind's attention actually works.

This is how the meditator's mindfulness awakening factor is supported by cessation.

When the meditator experiences the realm of neither-perception nor non-perception, and keeps opening and relaxing mind, eventually they will experience the Cessation of Perception, Feeling, and Consciousness (nirodha-samupatti).

During this occurrence, the meditator will not know this turning off of consciousness because they have no perception, feeling, or consciousness arising at all!

This is the only stage of meditation where this phenomenon occurs.

This meditation state is still mundane; it is not the Supramundane Nibbāna yet.

How can one know what is happening without perception, feeling, or consciousness?

It is only when the perception, feeling, and consciousness come back, and if mindfulness is sharp enough that the meditator will see directly each and every link of Dependent Origination arising, one by one as they occur.

However, even this is not the Supramundane State of Nibbāna.

The links they will see are:

> When _ignorance_ arises then formations arise;
> When _formations_ arise then consciousness arises;
> When _consciousness_ arises mentality-materiality arises; When mentality-materiality arises then the six-fold sense base arises;
> When the _six-fold sense base_ arises contact arises; when _contact_ arises feeling arises;
> When _feeling_ arises craving arises;
> When _craving_ arises then clinging arises;
> When _clinging_ arises then being arises;

When habitual tendency arises birth arises;
When birth arises then old age, death,
sorrow, lamentation, pain grief, and despair
arises.

This is how this whole mass of suffering
arises.

After this arising phenomenon ends, then the meditator will
experience the cessation of the links of Dependent
Origination, which happens like this.

With the remainderless fading away and
cessation of ignorance, formations cease;
When formations do not arise, consciousness
ceases;
When consciousness does not arise,
mentality/materiality cease;
When mentality/materiality does not arise,
the six-fold base ceases;
When the six-fold base does not arise,
contact ceases;
When contact does not arise, feeling ceases;
When feeling does not arise, craving ceases;
When craving does not arise, clinging ceases;
When clinging does not arise, habitual
tendencies (bhava) ceases;
When habitual tendencies (bhāva) do not
arise, birth ceases;
When birth does not arise, ageing and death,
sorrow, lamentation, pain, grief and despair
cease.

Thus is the cessation of this whole mass of
suffering and nibbāna occurs.

The seeing of Dependent Origination, both arising and ceasing, leads mind to the attainment of the "BIG OH WOW!" experience of the Supramundane Nibbāna.

The true understanding of precisely HOW Dependent Origination occurs is so profound that mind lets go of all concepts and the sign-less deliverance of mind—Nibbāna—occurs!

This is where a major change in the meditator's outlook and perspective occurs.

At that time, the meditator's mind becomes dispassionate about the belief in a permanent everlasting ego or self.

Through first hand experiential knowledge, the meditator sees and realizes that this is just an impersonal process and there is no one controlling the way phenomena arises and passes away.

These phenomena arise because conditions are right for them to arise.

In Buddhist terms, this is called 'anattā' or not-self nature of all existence.

The meditator also realizes that no one can possibly attain sainthood by the practice of mere chanting of words, using nimittas or phrases or suttas, or the practice of having rites and rituals done for them by someone else or by themselves.

The meditator has no more doubt about what is the correct path that leads to the higher stages of purity of mind and arahatship.

This is how a meditator becomes a sotāpanna and attains the true path of purification.

It is only through the realization of the Noble Truths by seeing Dependent Origination.

There is no other way to attain these exalted stages of understanding!

Although seeing these characteristics are a part of this realization, merely seeing the three characteristics by themselves will not now, nor ever be the experience, which leads to the Supramundane Nibbāna.

This is why all of the Buddha's appear in the world, to show the way to realizing the Four Noble Truths and seeing the true nature of How Dependent Origination is the key to freedom.

One develops the mindfulness awakening factor, which is supported by seclusion, dispassion, and cessation, which ripens in relinquishment.

One develops the investigation of experience awakening factor, which is supported by seclusion, dispassion, and cessation, which ripens in relinquishment.

One develops the energy awakening factor, which is supported by seclusion, dispassion, and cessation, which ripens in relinquishment.

One develops the joy awakening factor, which is supported by seclusion, dispassion, and cessation, which ripens in relinquishment.

One develops the tranquility awakening factor, which is supported by seclusion, dispassion, and cessation, which ripens in relinquishment.

One develops the collectedness awakening factor, which is supported by seclusion, dispassion, and cessation, which ripens in relinquishment.

One develops the equanimity awakening factor, which is supported by seclusion, dispassion, and cessation, which ripens in relinquishment.

43] "Monks that is how the Seven Awakening Factors, developed and cultivated, fulfill true knowledge and deliverance.

Since this sutta describes the Four Foundations of Mindfulness and the Seven Awakening Factors, the author will conclude with the last part of the Satipaṭṭhāna Sutta.

This is taken from the Majjhima Nikāya Sutta number 10, sections 46 to 47. It says:

46) Monks, if anyone should develop these Four Foundations of Mindfulness in such a way for seven years, one of two fruits could be expected for him: either final knowledge here and now, or if there is a trace of clinging left, non-return.

This means attaining to the state of being an Anāgāmī or non-returner

Let alone seven years, monks. If anyone should develop these four foundations of mindfulness in such a way for six years, one

of two fruits could be expected for him: either final knowledge here and now, or if there is a trace of clinging left, non-return.

Let alone seven years, monks. If anyone should develop these four foundations of mindfulness in such a way for six years

Let alone six years, monks. If anyone should develop these four foundations of mindfulness in such a way for five years, one of two fruits could be expected for him: either final knowledge here and now, or if there is a trace of clinging left, non-return.

Let alone five years, monks. If anyone should develop these four foundations of mindfulness in such a way for four years, one of two fruits could be expected for him: either final knowledge here and now, or if there is a trace of clinging left, non-return.

Let alone four years, monks. If anyone should develop these four foundations of mindfulness in such a way for three years, one of two fruits could be expected for him: either final knowledge here and now, or if there is a trace of clinging left, non-return.

Let alone three years, monks. If anyone should develop these four foundations of mindfulness in such a way for two years, one of two fruits could be expected for him: either final knowledge here and now, or if there is a trace of clinging left, non-return.

Let alone two years, monks. If anyone should develop these four foundations of mindfulness in such a way for one year, one of two fruits could be expected for him: either final knowledge here and now, or if there is a trace of clinging left, non-return.

Let alone one year, monks. If anyone should develop these Four Foundations of Mindfulness in such a way for seven months, one of two fruits could be expected for him: either final knowledge here and now, or if there is a trace of clinging left, non-return.

Let alone seven months, monks. If anyone should develop these four foundations of mindfulness in such a way for six months, one of two fruits could be expected for him: either final knowledge here and now, or if there is a trace of clinging left, non-return.

Let alone six months, monks. If anyone should develop these four foundations of mindfulness in such a way for five months, one of two fruits could be expected for him: either final knowledge here and now, or if there is a trace of clinging left, non-return.

Let alone five months, monks. If anyone should develop these four foundations of mindfulness in such a way for four months, one of two fruits could be expected for him: either final knowledge here and now, or if there is a trace of clinging left, non-return.

Let alone four months, monks. If anyone should develop these four foundations of mindfulness in such a way for three months, one of two fruits could be expected for him: either final knowledge here and now, or if there is a trace of clinging left, non-return.

Let alone three months, monks. If anyone should develop these four foundations of mindfulness in such a way for two months, one of two fruits could be expected for him: either final knowledge here and now, or if there is a trace of clinging left, non-return.

Let alone two months, monks. If anyone should develop these four foundations of mindfulness in such a way for one month, one of two fruits could be expected for him: either final knowledge here and now, or if there is a trace of clinging left, non-return.

Let alone one month, monks. If anyone should develop these four foundations of mindfulness in such a way for a half month, one of two fruits could be expected for him: either final knowledge here and now, or if there is a trace of clinging left, non-return.

Let alone half a month. If anyone should develop these Four Foundations of Mindfulness in such a way for seven days, one of two fruits could be expected for him: either final knowledge here and now, or if there is a trace of clinging left, non-return.

47) So, it was with reference to this that it was said:

'Monks, this is a 'direct path for the purification of beings, for the surmounting of sorrow and lamentation, for the disappearance of pain and grief, for the attainment of the true way, for the realization of Nibbāna - namely, the Four Foundations of Mindfulness. '"

That is what the Blessed One said. The monks were satisfied and delighted in the Blessed One's words.

This is a pretty big claim, which is not made up by the author.

He is only reporting what is in the suttas.

When a meditator is serious about the practice of developing their mind through the Tranquility of the Mindfulness of Breathing or the Mindfulness of Loving-Kindness, they can reach the final goal in this very lifetime.

When the meditator reaches the first pleasant abiding (the first jhāna), if they continue on with their practice, they have the potential to attain either the stage of "Anāgāmī" or "arahat."

This is what the Buddha said.

If a meditator is ardent, and continues without changing or stopping in their practice, then surely they will reach the goal, which is described.

Again, remember that the only way to attain the Supramundane Nibbāna is by realizing Dependent Origination both arising and ceasing.

There is no other way because this is the seeing and realizing of the Four Noble Truths, which forms the main teaching of the Buddha.

Great fruits and benefits befall on those who practiced according to the instructions prescribed by the Buddha.

SADHU. . .. SADHU. . .. SADHU. . ..

The sincere wish of the author is that all who practice meditation will continue on with their efforts until they reach the highest and best state possible, that is, the attainment of Final Liberation, the Supramundane Nibbāna.

May all those who are sincere, know, and understand the Four Noble Truths and through direct knowledge attain the highest goal.

May all practitioners of the Buddha's path, realize all of the links of Dependent Origination quickly, and easily; so that their suffering will soon be overcome.

Sharing of Merit

The author would like to share the merit accrued by the writing of this book with his mother and father, relatives, helpers, and all beings, so that they can eventually attain the highest Bliss and be free from all suffering!

May suffering ones be suffering free
And the fear struck fearless be
May the grieving shed all grief
And may all beings find relief.

May all beings share this merit

That we have thus acquired
For the acquisition of
all kinds of happiness.

May beings inhabiting space and earth
Devas and Nāgas of mighty power
Share in this merit of ours.

May they long protect
the Buddha's Dispensation.

Sadhu! Sadhu! Sadhu!

Footnotes

[1] The author refers to the Ānāpānasati Sutta, which includes the Four Foundations of Mindfulness, as well as the Seven Enlightenment Factors.

[2] See *Thus Have I Heard. The Long Discourses of the Buddha,* translated by Maurice Walsh, Wisdom Publications (1987), p.556.

[3] See Mahāsaccaka Sutta, sutta number 36 of Majjhima Nikāya.

[4] This means all nine of them! They are the four material jhānas, the four immaterial jhānas and the cessation of perception and feeling.

[5] Here, the word "jhāna" carries the meaning of absorption concentration (appaṇā samādhi), or access concentration (upacāra samādhi). This is the stage right before mind becomes absorbed into the object of meditation. These are the standard definitions as given teachers.

[6] In this context, it only means absorption (appaṇā samādhi) and not access concentration (upacāra samādhi).

[7] Some meditation teachers call this momentary concentration or moment-to-moment concentration (khanikha samādhi)

[8] Notice the plural form of the word "sutta"—this means seeing the agreement many times.

[9] This ceremony marks the end of the rains retreat where the Bhikkhus gathered together to confess any slight wrong doing which they many have committed.

[10] This refers to talking and idle gossip. The Bhikkhus waited patiently, and quietly doing their own meditation practices of expanding the silent mind and having clear mindfulness while waiting for the Buddha to speak.

[11] This refers to mindfulness of the body, mindfulness of feelings, mindfulness of consciousness, and mindfulness of mind objects.

[12] For example, see Mahāsakuludayi Sutta, Sutta Number 77 and Anupada Sutta, Sutta Number 111. Both of these suttas are found in the Majjhima Nikāya.

Glossary

A working terminology for the Tranquil Wisdom Insight Meditation (TWIM) practice as described in the suttas.

Buddhist Meditation shows us how mind's movements actually work.

It reveals the true nature of things by uncovering the moment-to-moment impersonal process of Dependent Origination, the Four Noble Truths, and the Three Characteristics of Existence.

The Buddha Dhamma specifically shows us HOW we get caught by suffering, how this first manifests, the exact cause of it and the way out.

The journey can sometimes be difficult but it also can be magical and fun as the changes become apparent in your life and people begin to notice the change for the good in you.

As we study this, we need to understand clearly some working definitions of certain training terminology.

From the beginning of our training the meditator learns to do this practice ALL OF THE TIME.

So, the precise definitions of terminology are very important if we are going to use this practice as our key to opening this doorway to Peace and these definitions may be slightly different from what you have heard in other places.

Before you begin to read further in this book, make sure the author and you are on the same page with key words for the training is pretty important.

This chapter has been put in the back of the book to assist the beginner and for solving any mix-up in understanding for the experienced practitioner.

The Definitions for terminology used in this book for training appear more or less in the order that you will have to deal with them as you learn the practice of Meditation.

Meditation (bhavana) - observing the movements of mind's attention moment-to-moment, object-to-object for the purpose of seeing clearly the impersonal process of Dependent Origination and the Four Noble Truths.

Mindfulness (sati) - 'Remembering' to observe the movements of mind's attention.

Awareness (sampajana) – *Understanding* what mind is doing; meaning whether it releasing what is arising, or getting involved with it? It is the true practicing of the 6R's – That is: *Recognizing* the movements of mind's attention, or is it moving into craving and clinging.

It is *Releasing, Relaxing, Re-smiling* and then *Returning* to the object of meditation to *Repeating* or continuing with mindfulness.

Object of Meditation – Any object of meditation we choose is to become the home-base for centering during our meditation.

The information we seek will not be found in the object of meditation we observe, but rather it is our recognition of the impersonal Process of Dependent Origination that leads to our knowledge and vision.

This occurs around the object of meditation.

Hindrances (nīvaraṇa) - unwholesome tendencies that begin with an arising feeling that is the same as any other feelings and should be treated in the same way during the meditation by practicing the 6R's - Releasing and relaxing them and not placing mind's attention on them in any way. By denying them mind's attention they will become weak and fade away.

Jhāna - The definition here of "**Jhāna**" in Buddhist terms is a *"stage of meditation through understanding (the interconnectedness of the* Four Noble Truths *and Dependent Origination) and seeing how mind actually works."* Level of understanding; stage of the meditation path

Craving (taṇhā) - the weak link in the process of Dependent Origination, which manifests as tension and tightness in mind and body as it is first appearing.

The common definition for the word Craving is "to want or desire," but there is much more to this word.

According to the Buddha there is a definite pattern with everything that arises. For instance, in order "to see" there is a set way things happen.

First, there must be a functioning sense door such as the eye.

Next there must be color and form.

When the eye hits color and form then eye-consciousness arises.

The meeting of these three things is called eye-contact.

With eye-contact as condition eye-feeling arises (Feeling [Vedanā] is pleasant, painful or neither painful nor pleasant and this is either physical or mental feeling.)

With eye-feeling as condition, then eye-craving arises.

Now "**Craving**" (taṇhā) in all of its many different forms (seeing, hearing, tasting, smelling, bodily sensations, and thoughts) always arises as being a tensions and tightness in both mind and body.

"Craving" (taṇhā) also always manifests as the *"I like it" or "I don't like it"* mind and can be recognized as tension or tightness in both one's mind and body.

This is where we come to understand the importance of the Buddha's instructions about consciously tranquilizing one's mind and body.

When the meditator has any kind of distraction arising, that pulls their attention away from their object of meditation, then a feeling immediately arises, and next, right after that the **"*I like it.... I don't like it*" [craving-taṇhā] mind arises.**

This is seen sometimes as a big gross tightness and sometimes as a very subtle tightness or tension in mind and body.

As **"Craving"** (taṇhā) is the cause of suffering (the Second Noble Truth) what the meditator must do is softly let go of that tension or tightness (i.e. relax, and this must consciously be done. It doesn't happen automatically as it is shown in the meditation instruction given to us by the Buddha), then smile, and gently redirect mind's attention back to the object of meditation (this *step* is the Third Noble Truth or the cessation of craving or suffering).

In practical terms, this relaxing is the most important and major step that the Buddha discovered, this and the Fourth Noble Truth—that is the way' leading to the Cessation of Suffering.

The Buddha saw that when "Craving" (taṇhā) was let go of; mind became clear, open, very observant, and pure.

He saw that the thinking and conceptualizing mind did not arise.

The thinking and conceptualizing mind in Buddhism is called "Clinging" (Upādāna).

So, when a teacher says something like *"Cling to Nothing,"* they are actually saying to "stop thinking about things and just observe,", which is good advice as far as it goes.

Actually it would be better to say *"Crave Nothing,"* but that would be misunderstood because how are we supposed to do that?

"Crave Nothing" means "to notice and let go of the tightness or tension in one's mind and body before it arises."

How does one do this?

When one sees a "Feeling" arise, *if they relax* at that very moment, then the "Craving" (taṇhā) won't arise.

"Craving" (taṇhā) is the weak link in the cycle or process of Dependent Origination.

It CAN be recognized and let go of, and when it is released then the "Clinging" (Upādāna) won't arise.

One thing that has become popular today is the putting together of these two words, **"Craving/Clinging"** and I think it helps to cause even more confusion.

"Craving" is the "I like it ... I don't like it" mind and "Clinging" is all of the thoughts, ideas, opinions, and concepts why mind likes or dislikes a feeling when it arises.

They are two very different and separate parts to the process of how things work.

So putting them together just makes one's understanding of this process even cloudier. Some teachers today are trying to say the **"Craving and Clinging"** can be best defined as **"Grasping."**

And as the author just explained that moves away from the more precise definitions that the Buddha shows us within his teaching.

No-self (anattā) - Impersonal Nature; Impersonal perspective. An absence of taking anything personally, which occurs during life.

Seeing things purely as they are without the arising of craving is the beginning of anattā.

To do this in life, you don't have to stop using the pronouns in your language! And you don't have to try to disappear. Promise.

Delusion (moha) – In some Buddhist traditions the word "Delusion" (Moha) is linked up with two other words, which are **"Lust"** (lobha) and **"Hatred"** (dosa).

Together these three words are sometimes called "the three poisons."

This actually is a reasonable way to look at them.

But there is some confusion about what "Delusion" (Moha) actually means.

The Buddha meant something a little bit different every time he used this word.

According to the suttas the word "Delusion" (Moha) means to see whatever arises as being a personal self (attā).

Or we can say that "Delusion" (Moha) is seeing things through the false (deluded) idea of a self (attā).

In other words, one takes all feelings or sensations to be a part of the "I," "Me," "My," "Mine" (attā) identification, that is Delusion.

Serenity (samatha) - Here again is another word to look at.

In Pāli the word is **Samatha**.

The meaning of Samatha is tranquility, serenity, peacefulness, stillness, or collectedness.

Often the common popular definition is a strongly one-pointed type of concentration, absorption concentration, or ecstatic concentration.

This specific definition of serenity or tranquility certainly implies a different type of "collectedness" than the deeper types of absorption or ecstatic concentration.

The goal of absorption or ecstatic concentration is to have mind stay on only one thing as if it were glued to it (to the exclusion of anything else).

The Samatha Collectedness implies to have a mind that is still, serene, calm, and collected—a mind that is very alert to whatever shifting or moving mind's attention does moment-to-moment.

Of course Samatha/Vipassanā (which is the standard way it is described in the suttas where they are always linked together) leads to the total Liberation of mind by seeing and recognizing how the Four Noble Truths interact with Dependent Origination.

As the Bodhisatta found out firsthand, Samatha/Vipassanā leads directly to the end-result of Nibbāna and absorption or ecstatic concentration does not.

Insight (vipassanā) – This word has a surface meaning, which is "seeing things as they truly are."

According to the Buddha, the definition goes much deeper than that. **"Insight"** or understanding into what?

Insight refers to "realizing the impersonal nature and deeply understanding of the Four Noble Truths and HOW Dependent Origination actually occurs with everything that arises and passes away (anicca) in one's mind and body."

In other words, one gains a deeper and deeper understanding (in each stage of Jhāna) of the impersonal process of *HOW* mind and body arises through truly seeing and understanding (knowledge and vision) of the Four Noble Truths interconnection with the ongoing processes of Dependent Origination.

When one can see clearly these processes in all of existence, they will experience an unshakable knowledge that this is the right path to follow.

Mind's attention begins to see clearly that whatever arises and passes away (anicca) is a part of a definite process and this leads to a deep understanding that everything going on is a part of an impersonal pattern (anattā).

These **"Insights"** can occur at any time whether one is sitting in meditation or doing their daily activities.

They are quite profound when they occur.

'Insights' are like finding a lost part to a puzzle and this is where the true "aha!" experiences happen.

Wisdom (paññā) – there are many phrases within the suttas using the word 'wisdom' and they usually turn out, in some context or other, to be concerning "the impersonal process of Dependent Origination."

Anytime the words "**Wise Attention**" or "**Wisdom**" is seen in the suttas they are referring to the understanding of the Four Noble Truths and the process of Dependent Origination. Other such phrases appear as:

"**He sees with Wisdom,**"" **Seeing with Wisdom,**" "**And his taints were destroyed by his seeing with Wisdom,**" "**Wisdom,**" or "**He is Wise.**"

If we can remember these instances are referring to understanding the Four Noble Truths and seeing clearly the process of Dependent Origination as we read the various suttas, then our minds will open up to a new understanding of how this process and the Four Noble Truths uncover the core of the teaching of the Buddha.

Concentration (samādhi) - The Pāli word actually means the unification or bringing together of mind.

The word "Collectedness" appears to be more functional for success in the meditation rather than the word "Concentration."

Here in the West people take the word *"Concentration"* to mean a kind of deep, one-pointedness of mind or an absorbed mind, and this is not what the Buddha was trying to get across.

Before the time of the Buddha there were many words that described deep absorption or one-pointedness of mind.

But the Buddha made up a new word "Samādhi" to describe a completely different way of seeing and experiencing the Jhāna.

After the Buddha's parinibbāna, because this word was very popular, the Brahmins of that time changed the definition of "Samādhi" back to mean "strong one-pointedness."

But, the Buddha was showing that there is a difference between a 'Collected Mind' and a strongly absorbed or 'Concentrated Mind'.

The words "Collected Mind"' (Samādhi) gives us the idea of a mind that is composed, calm, still, very alert, and pure, because one has let go of craving.

This kind of mind observes HOW mind's attention shifts from one thing to another.

A "Concentrated"' mind, on the other hand, means that mind is stuck on one thing to the exclusion of anything else that may try to arise.

So a "Concentrated"' Mind by this definition loses full awareness and mindfulness (Sati) of what is happening in the present moment because it is only seeing the one thing it is pointing at.

This statement also refers to "access or neighborhood concentration" (Upacāra Samādhi) and "moment-to-moment concentration" (Khaṇikha Samādhi). Why?

The simple answer is, there is no tranquilizing of mind and body before the meditator brings their attention back to the object of meditation.

Because of this, there is no seeing of how the Four Noble Truths and Dependent Origination actually work and how craving (tightness and tension) is brought back to the meditation object.

This is why when the teachers of straight "**Vipassanā**" tell their students that *Absorption Concentration* won't ever lead to Nibbāna, they are 100% correct.

Any kind of practice, which divides "**Samatha Meditation**" and "**Vipassanā Meditation**" into two different practices, can't possibly lead one to Nibbāna. Why?

Because mind has the need to be calm, composed, and clear, while it is in a jhāna, in order to see clearly the interconnectedness of the Four Noble Truths and Dependent Origination.

This is why the practice of straight vipassanā has led to so much disappointment after so many years of hard work for some students.

The Buddha taught us to practice "**Samatha/Vipassanā**" together and this is the difference between commentary-based meditation practices and the Sutta approach to meditation.

The results of these two practices are different.

One-pointed *Concentration*' or absorption concentration is not the same kind of mental development that the Buddha shows us.

The Buddha taught us to tranquilize our mind and body every time mind's attention shifts from one thing to another.

The *Collected Mind* is not so deeply one-pointed that the force of one's *Concentration*' causes mind to stay on one object of meditation, even if that attention Concentrates on something momentarily.

The Collected Mind is able to observe how mind's attention goes from one thing to another, very precisely.

There is much more full awareness of both mind and body here than with a deeply *Concentrated*' one-pointed mind or absorbed mind.

This is why I choose to use the word *Collected* rather than *Concentrated* mind.

By using the word Collected there is less confusion about the kind of meditation that the Buddha is referring to and it is easier to understand the descriptions given in the suttas.

These words are a good start for you to work with this approach to the meditation.

Bhante Vimalaraṁsi's Background

Bhante Vimalaraṁsi became a Buddhist monk in 1986, because of his keen interest in meditation.

He went to Burma in 1988 to practice intensive mediation at the famous meditation center, Mahāsi Yeiktha in Rangoon.

There he practiced meditation for 20 to 22 hours a day for almost a year, then because of some social unrest, all foreigners were asked to leave the country, so Bhante went to Malaysia and practiced intensive Loving-kindness meditation for 6 months.

In 1990, Bhante went back to Burma for more intensive "Vipassanā" meditation, for 16 hours a day, at Chanmyay Yeiktha in Rangoon.

He practiced for 2 years, sometimes sitting in meditation for as long as 7 to 8 hours a sitting.

After two years of intensive meditation and experiencing what they said was the final result, he became very disillusioned with the Vipassanā method and left Burma to continue his search.

He went back to Malaysia and began teaching loving-kindness meditation.

In 1995, Bhante was invited to live and teach at the largest Theravādan monastery in Malaysia by the Venerable K Sri Dhammananada.

This Sri Lankan monastery offered public talks every Friday evening and Sunday morning where 300 to 500 people would attend.

Bhante gave talks every other Friday and on every Sunday.

While staying there he had the opportunity to meet many learned monks, and Bhante questioned them at length about the Buddha's teachings.

He found out that the Vipassanā method of meditation is taken from a commentary written a thousand years after the Buddha's death.

This commentary is not very accurate when compared with the original teachings.

Bhante Vimalaraṁsi then began to study the original texts and practice meditation according to these texts.

After a three month self-retreat, he came back to Malaysia and wrote a book on Mindfulness of Breathing called "The Ānāpānasati Sutta-A Practical Guide to Mindfulness of Breathing and Tranquil Wisdom Insight Meditation."

There are now over 600,000 copies distributed worldwide in seven languages.

This book is currently used as a practical study guide by some schools of religion, meditation teachers and their students.

Bhante Vimalaraṁsi came back to the U.S. in 1998 and has been teaching meditation throughout the country since then.

In 2003, along with a well-known Venerable Paññāloka Mahāthera, Bhante Vimalaraṁsi founded a non-profit corporation called United International Buddha Dhamma Society (UIBDS) and set up initial location of the Dhamma Sukha Meditation Center in Missouri. An online support group was built to offer ongoing help to students who attended retreats.

In 2004 the first website was constructed for a new outreach program and to attempt to spread Dhamma talks online. In 2006, the first novice ordination happened on the land and a yearly retreat began in Joshua Tree, CA at the Dhamma Dena Vipassanā Center.

By 2006 Venerable was selected by his peers to become the First Representative to the World Buddhist Conference in Japan dedicated to the investigation of Foundation Buddhism. This is the first American Buddhist Temple and study center on American Soil where all the teaching is done by monastics using English as the primary communicative language.

In 2008 Venerable attended the Dedication of the Royal Grand Hall of Buddhism in Kato, Japan. In his speech he officially announced the founding of the "Buddhist American Forest Tradition".

In 2009 the support list had grown to over 450 members and the Website many helpers around the world who were translating into 7 different languages various parts of that site. There were now nearly 100 talks online available to listen to and to study.

In recent years the center in Missouri is receiving notable Venerables from various countries to visit and learn more about what is happening with this practice. They want to understand how to teach it so people in their own country can learn it. The center sits on 102 acres of land with 6 cabins for practitioners and several huts for monastics. Larger buildings, such as the kitchen and dining hall and Dhamma Hall have been completed and planning for a memorial shrine to the late Most Venerable U Silananda, and a new Women's residence and study area are in a planning phase.

2011 the new dining hall and meditation study area and library complex was finished at long last. It is a beautiful building in a "log cabin" style with high ceilings and large windows. A tornado hit the old lower house and monastics area, but it allowed us to rebuild the area and modernize the buildings.

In 2012 we welcomed the new beautiful eight-sided Meditation Hall building so finally, at long last, our facility now will provide a safe and secure area in which to practice. Embedded in the wall are Quartz crystals as well as the foundation is laid with meditative stones.

Students and many other people are now showing interest around the world.

Venerable Vimalaraṁsi lives mainly in the Forest Retreat Center in Annapolis, MO, which in time will become an International location where monks may come to improve their English and study more deeply the TWIM meditation and this approach to Sutta studies.

Support for DSMC may be sent to:
United International Buddha Dhamma Society Inc.

Donations are tax deductible.

UIBDS
c/o Dhamma Sukha Meditation Center
8218 County Road # 204, Annapolis, MO 63620
USA

The Gift of Dhamma is the highest and best gift.

Dhamma Sukha Meditation Center
Anāthapiṇḍika's Park Complex
8218 County Road # 204
Annapolis, MO 63620
URL: www.dhammasukha.org

Made in the USA
Coppell, TX
15 March 2021

51774003R00184